POTTERY BARN

livingrooms

TEXT
bonnie schwartz

PHOTOGRAPHY
alan williams

STYLING
michael walters

EXECUTIVE EDITOR
clay ide

Oxmoor House®

Oxmoor House®

Oxmoor House books are distributed by Sunset Books
80 Willow Road, Menlo Park, CA 94025

Oxmoor House and Sunset Books are divisions of
Southern Progress Corporation

SUNSET BOOKS

Vice President, General Manager Rich Smeby
Vice President, Editorial Director Bob Doyle
National Account Manager Brad Moses

POTTERY BARN

President Laura Alber
Senior Vice President, Design & Product Development Celia Tejada
Vice President, Creative Services Clay Ide
Editor Samantha Moss
Photo Coordinator, Special Projects Gina Risso

WELDON OWEN

Chief Executive Officer John Owen
President Terry Newell
Chief Operating Officer Larry Partington
Vice President, International Sales Stuart Laurence

Creative Director Gaye Allen
Vice President, Publisher Roger Shaw
Business Manager Richard Van Oosterhout

Associate Publisher Shawna Mullen
Art Director Emma Boys
Managing Editor Peter Cieply
Production Director Chris Hemesath
Color Manager Teri Bell
Photo Coordinator Elizabeth Lazich

Pottery Barn Living Rooms was conceived and produced by
Weldon Owen Inc.
814 Montgomery Street, San Francisco, CA 94133
in collaboration with Pottery Barn
3250 Van Ness Avenue, San Francisco, CA 94109

Set in Simoncini Garamond™ and Formata™

Color separations by AGT—Seattle
Printed in Singapore by Tien Wah Press (Pte.) Ltd.

A WELDON OWEN PRODUCTION

First printed 2003
10 9 8 7 6 5 4

Library of Congress Control Number 2003106154
ISBN 0-8487-2759-2

The Heart of Your Home

What is it about our homes that we love? Naturally, they fulfill our most basic desires for warmth, shelter, and security. They also reflect our truest feelings about what's important to us. The living room is a place to work, relax, and play. It's also the room where friends and family come together, so it has to be an inviting place to linger. Furnished with comfort and style, a living room can be a place of refuge at the heart of your home.

At Pottery Barn, we're devoted to the idea that your home can be an endless source of inspiration. We believe that decorating with style should be easy and fun, and a large part of our mission is to demystify interior decorating. We design our furnishings to work in many different spaces, and we fill our catalogs with inventive, achievable ideas. This book is full of inspiration and tips we've gleaned from decorating more than five thousand rooms during the past ten years. We shoot all our photography in real homes, often in one day, so our ideas must always be accessible and easy to accomplish. What we've learned over the years is that any room, anywhere, offers unique creative opportunities. We believe your home should be an expression of you, your family, and your lifestyle. In *Pottery Barn Living Rooms*, you'll see how easy it can be to create a welcoming space with a special sense of style that's completely your own.

THE POTTERY BARN DESIGN TEAM

contents

your style

The living room is, by definition, the space in a home that's most full of life and spirit. This is the place that accommodates the widest range of activities important to you and your family. It is a room for solitude and gathering, for working and playing, for memories recalled and those in the making.

Turning your living room into an oasis from the world outside is not difficult to achieve. But before you order a coffee table or pick up a paintbrush, look at your space with an objective eye. Whether you're redesigning the whole room or

When choosing furniture and accessories, start with the basics: a comfortable, well-made sofa, a versatile coffee table, a quality rug, and simple, beautiful drapes. Then build from there. With quality furnishings, you can be fearless about choosing the items you wish to display. You'll also have the option of changing the room's design with different accents to keep it lively, allowing you to evolve your style over time.

Creating a room that adapts easily is a cinch if you incorporate furniture into your space that can be used in different ways. A card table can be

A living room expresses a sense of welcome and sets the tone for the rest of your home. Design yours to receive all who enter with comfort and style.

just refreshing it for a party, open your mind to the creative possibilities; think about furniture and finishes, color and texture, scent and sound.

Most of all, follow your own instincts. What's important is not a certain style, but your style: what is right for you? Choose furniture, materials, and colors that inspire you. If you love cozy spaces, carve out a private nook with a daybed and a jumble of pillows where you can read or nap. If you're drawn to the daylight that washes across a specific part of the room, arrange a comfortable sitting area there. Trusting your own eye for and feelings about decor will generate the best ideas for decorating *your* living room.

put to work as a serving table for hors d'oeuvres during a party; an oversized ottoman can also serve as a coffee table; a trunk can be used both as an end table and as extra storage for everything from blankets to board games.

A living room is a place where both family and friends should feel instantly at home. Decorate yours in a way that allows everyone to use and enjoy it more. The living room is the threshold between public and private life, so strike a chord that embraces both and resonates through your entire home. Create a space that's approachable, casual, and comfortable, and no matter how you furnish it, your room will always be full of life.

Room for Living

The living room is a gathering place, a space that embraces family and friends with relaxed style. The best living spaces communicate warmth with an undercurrent of playfulness, starting with a framework of solid basics and employing good design on a large, welcoming scale.

Creating a family-friendly living room with areas for reading, talking, working, and relaxing not only enriches the room, it enriches your life. A living room that invites many varied activities into its space ensures that family members can do their own thing and yet spend time happily together, whether tackling homework on weeknights or reading the paper on Sunday mornings.

This easy-living weekend home is a perfect example. It's flexible in organization, appealingly tactile, and open to all. Attractive and practical elements all function in more than one way to ensure that the room works well and is a creative place to be. A sense of uncluttered abundance is the key: all that's needed is present and plentiful, yet organized in a way that keeps the space open and livable.

Classic, versatile furniture is the best foundation for keeping a living room comfortable and up-to-date. It's then easy to add a slipcover in velvet for the holidays, for instance, or new pillows and throws, instead of redecorating the entire room. Establishing a neutral palette and accenting it with bold dashes of color allows flexibility in decorating.

Enliven a neutral backdrop, *left*, with an infusion of strong color. Red and black accents – pillows, throws, fresh flowers, and artwork – stimulate the eye and offset the white walls, brown leather upholstery, and warm wood tones. **A chalkboard-topped coffee table**, *right*, offers an outlet for creativity and communicates a casual style and a lighthearted sense of fun.

A large, open space can feel warm and cozy when it's grounded by an abundance of smaller-scaled objects and soft pillows. Dashes of more formal elements, like a chandelier and gallery-framed photos, add richness.

Separating the living space from the kitchen with a long dining table breaks this room into comfortable zones. An out-of-the-ordinary table is fitted with wheels, allowing even more versatility in the room's arrangement.

Make a virtue of storage, *above*, to add color and style to a room while keeping things organized and close at hand. **A linen-covered sectional sofa**, *right*, is fashioned for flexibility out of four separate futons. Red hanging lamps help zone the room and offer a vibrant transition to the dining area, where a chalkboard menu and dinner bell set the tone for celebration.

A living room can be stylish and still invite relaxation. Versatile furnishings create comfort and allow you to keep decor up-to-date.

A well-designed living room can be informal, yet sophisticated enough for special occasions. In a large space such as this second-home great room, a generous sectional sofa offers optimal flexibility. It invites everything from quick naps to overnight guests and can be rearranged into different seating areas. Plenty of pillows make it comfortable and simple to dress for entertaining. The clever coffee table on wheels is easily moved or rolled out of sight when not in use.

A single bold accent color or an unexpected material goes a long way toward making a quiet room sparkle. Here, bright red calls attention to the natural subtlety of linen and wood surfaces around it. The chalkboard table encourages spontaneity.

A framed flat-screen TV, *left*, echoes dramatic black-framed photographs and becomes an unobtrusive part of the room when not in use. **A craft table**, *right*, allows the family to work and play together. Creative storage ideas – stacked vintage cigar boxes for supplies, an old toy truck filled with CDs – make this work area attractive.

Design Details

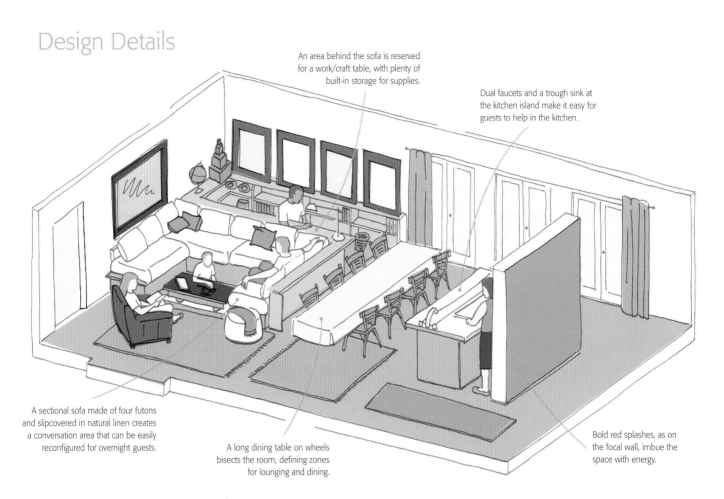

An area behind the sofa is reserved for a work/craft table, with plenty of built-in storage for supplies.

Dual faucets and a trough sink at the kitchen island make it easy for guests to help in the kitchen.

A sectional sofa made of four futons and slipcovered in natural linen creates a conversation area that can be easily reconfigured for overnight guests.

A long dining table on wheels bisects the room, defining zones for lounging and dining.

Bold red splashes, as on the focal wall, imbue the space with energy.

Color Palette

A bold contemporary color scheme of white, red, and black creates drama in this sunny living room. The bright red is used sparingly in room materials — on the focal wall and the hanging lamps, for example — and also in accessories like the sofa pillows. Natural linen upholstery and unfinished pine-plank floors temper the palette, add a natural appeal, and infuse the large space with warmth.

Room Plan

Zoned according to different uses, this large room accommodates a wide variety of activities, from food preparation to art projects, and from communal dining to private conversations. A simple palette and plenty of built-in storage keep the room looking trim and organized. A casual arrangement of gallery-framed photos and art create a themed wall display. A large, flat-screen TV attached to the wall has a simple black frame built around it, helping it to blend into the room and become a piece of artwork itself.

Materials

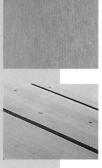

Jute This fiber derived from the stalk of an Indian herb is woven to make rugs that are durable, stain resistant, and ideal for high-traffic areas.

Linen Woven from the fibers of the flax plant, this crisp and cool fabric is twice as strong as cotton and softens with washing and use.

Pine While pine tends to be a soft wood, white pine, one of the harder species of this coniferous family, is used for floors, trim, and cabinetwork.

space

The space in a room is naturally set by its boundaries and by the arrangement of its furniture. But space is also the impression a room offers. It is the room's very character, and influences all aspects of its design. The way you choose to arrange and style your space determines how large or intimate, how cool or warm, and how restful or active it will feel.

Thinking about traffic flow in a busy living space is one key to making it comfortable. Consider how you move through the room internally as well as from this room to others,

Large rooms can be zoned to seem more intimate; small ones can gain a sense of spaciousness with simple styling. Make the most of a room that has low ceilings or an unusual shape by bringing in richly colored pillows and throws to fashion a cozy retreat. Paint architectural details the same color as the walls to create a uniform backdrop, or call attention to them by making them focal points or natural space dividers.

Light and color, too, transform a space. The intensity of lighting and depth of hues you choose affect the way a room makes you feel.

The right design makes a living room more than the sum of its parts. Think of how you use the room, then shape the space to best suit the way you live.

and from inside to out. How do you want these transitions to feel? You might prefer an open-plan design where multiple activities can go on at once, or a layout with a single focus, such as two sofas placed facing each other by a fireplace to encourage conversation. Well-planned furniture placement can draw attention to specific areas or can create a sense that one may wander freely.

A good space plan guides you effortlessly from setting to setting: a place for family and friends to gather in comfort, a niche for quiet reading or daydreaming. With creative planning, your living room can graciously accommodate you and your lifestyle, whatever the shape of the space.

A space that's light all around offers an airy atmosphere; darker spaces feel snug. Dark walls and a light floor produce a floating sensation, whereas light walls and a dark floor draw attention upward yet ground a room comfortably.

The best way to begin planning your space is to look at each part of the room as a potential setting: groupings for entertaining, corners for solitude, mantels for display, floors for kids at play. Then think about the details, the little extras you can bring to the space to enhance each area and give it your personal touch. With this approach, your living room will become much more than its four walls and furniture.

Rooms Within a Room

A living space as "great room" needs to be many rooms at once: home theater, game room, and library, plus a place for everyday entertaining and quiet relaxation. The best layout of space in living rooms large or small is one that carves out flexible zones suited to different uses.

A spacious, open-plan living room is a luxury many of us dream about. High ceilings, bold architecture, lots of light, and room to roam – the living room as great room is a modern ideal borrowed from the grand estates of the past. Unlike its formal predecessors, today's great room is founded on casual comfort, and the challenge is to make it as personal and welcoming as possible.

For a great room to become a true gathering place, it needs areas where both intimate and large groups can feel at home. This may sound difficult, but it needn't be. You can unify even the largest living room by using light, color, and texture to create harmony among different areas. Take lessons from public spaces, like hotel lobbies and bistros. Each incorporates smaller zones for relaxing, conversing, or dining, yet functions as an attractive, seamless whole. The space in a living room can be similarly zoned.

To create a sense of spaciousness, paint walls a light color so they recede visually, emphasizing the room's height. Bring in natural wood and texture – chenille throws, cotton slipcovers, leather pillows – to keep the space feeling warm.

Create an intimate nook within a large room, *left*, for everyday lounging. This comfortable corner with its built-in window seat is ideal for reading or napping. Soft oversized cotton-covered pillows lend a sense of coziness, even in this high-ceilinged space. **A primitive rocker**, *right*, with books stacked to form a side table, offers another quiet spot for introspection.

In this room, transparent furnishings and accessories, like the glass coffee table, vases, and hurricane candle holders, emphasize spaciousness. Leaving windows bare opens things up further, inviting the outside in and bathing the room in light. Mirrors also help a room feel expansive; at the same time, they can bring focus to an area within a larger room.

Opaque objects can help define areas of intimacy. Flooring with a sheen reflects light across the space and encourages people to move through it; carpeted areas take on more of a sense of terra firma, places to gravitate toward and settle in. Using boundaries of carpeted areas on bare floor, you can subtly suggest a room within a room, and create a special place to read and rest.

A graceful handblown Spanish wine jug, *above*, becomes an informal sculpture. Grouping the jug with a linen-framed photograph and ceramic bowl adds layers of contrasting texture, and a provocative interplay between matte and polished, translucent and opaque. **Generous sofas**, *right*, topped with leather pillows become inviting places to sink in and rest. Pairing two creates a focused conversation area centered on the fireplace.

Simple furniture arrangements keep zones easy to reconfigure for gatherings of different sizes. The secret lies in having a variety of versatile pieces that you can use in unexpected ways.

A focal point – a singular object, an unusual shape, a bold contrast of texture or color – makes even quiet spaces come alive.

Repurposing things you love – like turning a rustic armoire into an entertainment center – brings warm, personal interest to a living room. Thinking creatively about furnishings and their uses can inspire ideas for unconventional furniture choices and practical and flexible arrangements.

Books stacked as an impromptu table, a classic modern chair (or a primitive handcrafted one) that does double duty as a sculpture, or a giant Spanish wine bottle used as a vase all help to shape space and anchor zones.

Framed by a clean, comfortable environment, *left*, classic designs like this Charles and Ray Eames molded plywood chair stand out as artworks. **An oversized antique armoire**, *right*, topped with a collection of sculptural black vessels, helps to define a discrete reading nook.

A pair of plump sofas cozy up to a glass table for evenings by the fire or entertaining family and friends. A looped wool rug defines the space and complements the knotty pine floor.

Design Details

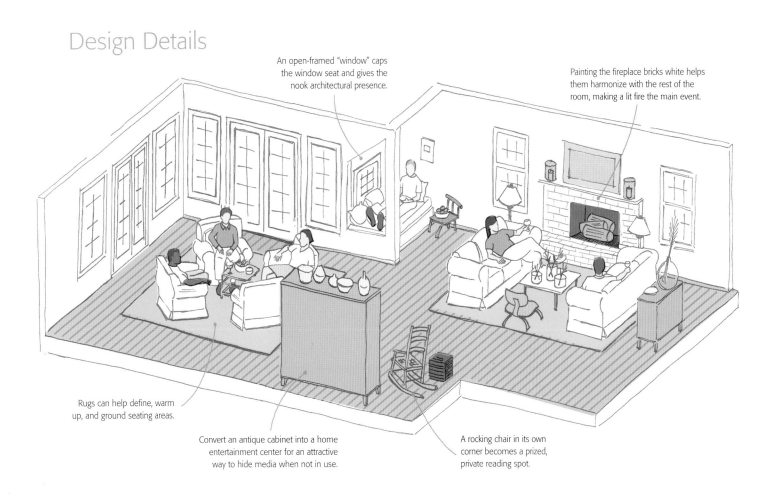

An open-framed "window" caps the window seat and gives the nook architectural presence.

Painting the fireplace bricks white helps them harmonize with the rest of the room, making a lit fire the main event.

Rugs can help define, warm up, and ground seating areas.

Convert an antique cabinet into a home entertainment center for an attractive way to hide media when not in use.

A rocking chair in its own corner becomes a prized, private reading spot.

Color Palette

A palette of creamy white, taupe, and honey creates a warm, easy-to-relax-in setting in this spacious great room. Often called a universal tone, taupe is a grayed brown that ranges from pale to dark and harmonizes with most other hues. Here, the taupe rug, white walls, and white upholstery form a neutral canvas against which various wood tones stand out, adding soothing hues from nature. White keeps the space feeling fresh and airy.

Room Plan

Rugs create the illusion of rooms within a room. Two sofas facing each other across a shared rug provide a comfortable conversation area. A group of four chairs on another rug serves as an alternate conversation zone or a place for quiet reading. A daybed nestled within a corner window offers a generous surface for afternoon naps or overnight guests. Choosing a coffee table and accessories that are transparent allows the room's abundant light to reflect throughout the space, maintaining an open feeling.

Materials

Pine planks This popular flooring option has a rustic quality. The knottier the pine and the wider the plank, the more rustic a room feels.

Cotton sailcloth This strong woven canvas, which resists stretching, moisture, and tearing, is a good choice for hardwearing upholstery.

Wool rug A flat-weave, looped wool rug is naturally soil resistant, so it makes a durable floor covering for high-traffic areas.

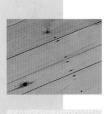

Making the Most of a Small Space

Overcoming a shortage of space is one of the most common challenges in decorating. With strategic design, even a modest room can reveal greatness. The secret to success lies in thoughtful organization of space and a simple color palette brought to life with creative flair.

Small living rooms, like camping trips, should be well planned and well provisioned. This is especially true in cottages, where the living room is the heart and soul – and sometimes nearly all there is – of the house. The space must be adaptable enough for just about anything, from dining and entertaining to working or watching TV. In the room shown here, lots of innovative storage, milk-white walls, and savvy furniture placement emphasize the curl-up nature of cottage living, and work to make the space feel larger.

The shape of a room determines its best arrangement. To zone a small living room, you can arrange welcoming seating at one end (where family and friends can linger and talk) and a multifunctional table at the other. Use walls and corners to do the hard work, employing adjustable shelving units to stash TVs, stereos, books, and tableware. Link the areas together with plenty of seating that can be moved from one place to another. You can also increase apparent space in a room by leaving windows bare and painting the walls and ceiling the same color.

Shelving tucked into the wall, *left*, maximizes space and stores all things useful and decorative, including antique silverware displayed in a trophy and napkin rings kept in a glass apothecary jar. **Keeping walls unadorned**, *right*, expands the sense of space; the mantel takes over as the main display area for layered artwork, photos, found objects, and special mementos. Denim slipcovers are washable and practical for multipurpose seating.

You don't have to choose between function and decor, even in a small space. Farm benches can be stacked for ad hoc shelving and taken apart if extra seating is needed. Chests can serve as coffee or side tables and can double as storage containers, keeping the space neat.

Let your cottage living room become a personal scrapbook, with furniture and accessories that are the accumulations of a meaningful life. Vintage items drafted into everyday use bring charm and warmth to the decor of a space-challenged room without adding clutter.

Good organization always adds to a room's appeal, but the difference between orderly and spare can be an artful balance in a tight space. Fill even a small room with useful accessories. They're the source of a design's warmth, the pleasure that comes from the nearness of favorite things. Possessions on display and rich colors all around turn a small room into a little gem.

A silver creamer, *above left*, adds elegance to a feather collection. **Turn flea market finds,** *left*, into innovative and decorative storage: an old tartanware-style lunch box and a 45-rpm record case keep papers organized; the lamp is a repurposed souvenir bottle. **A wood plank dining table,** *right*, doubles as a work surface for food preparation for the small kitchen. Denim, ticking, and painted wicker support the small room's casual, laid-back feel.

Cottage style is about making the most of the things you love. Rearrange favorite furniture often to keep the decor feeling fresh and active.

An old sea captain's chest is used as a coffee table, and a wooden shipping crate is set on a metal stand to become an end table. A wire cage lamp adds a witty touch. Matelassé and striped ticking pillows augment the comfortable seating.

Design Details

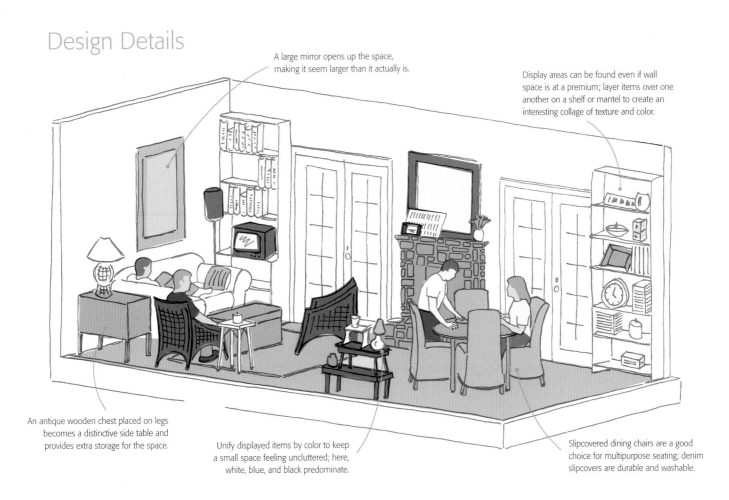

A large mirror opens up the space, making it seem larger than it actually is.

Display areas can be found even if wall space is at a premium; layer items over one another on a shelf or mantel to create an interesting collage of texture and color.

An antique wooden chest placed on legs becomes a distinctive side table and provides extra storage for the space.

Unify displayed items by color to keep a small space feeling uncluttered; here, white, blue, and black predominate.

Slipcovered dining chairs are a good choice for multipurpose seating; denim slipcovers are durable and washable.

Color Palette

A white, blue, and black palette, tempered by natural pine floors, makes this cottage a classic country retreat. Chairs slipcovered in blue denim and a blue cotton rug blend neatly with this living room's black accessories and woods. Blue is a color that fades beautifully, making it a wise choice for fabrics or rugs exposed to full sunlight. Uplifting white upholstery, ceilings, and walls balance the indigo and black tones.

Room Plan

Because this small room serves many functions, efficient storage is essential. Built-in shelves hold necessities such as cutlery, cookware, reading materials, and home entertainment equipment. A fieldstone fireplace separates the lounging area from the dining/cooking/work zone and becomes the focal point of both. Furniture serves double duty. Stacked, wooden benches become whimsical shelving for books and tableware; unstacked, they offer extra seating. Coffee and side tables, converted from old trunks and shipping boxes, also provide storage.

Materials

Board-and-batten An early form of residential siding, board-and-batten paneling is inexpensive and can be used to cover a whole house or as a decorative accent.

Fieldstone Found in fields where bedrock is close to the surface, fieldstone links a home to its surroundings.

Wicker Created with a technique of weaving vines, twigs, or branches around a coarser frame, wicker furnishings can stand up to a century of normal use.

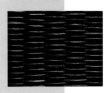

How to Work with Space

You can manipulate a room's space to look larger or cozier than it might otherwise appear. Using color, light, and furniture placement, try creating effects that seem to change the room's very shape. Whether you'd like to link one room to another or define obvious spatial distinctions, color and light are two of the most useful tools for changing how your space is perceived. Strong color contrasts like black and white visually divide space. Low contrasts like those used in neutral or monochromatic schemes emphasize spaciousness. Employ techniques that draw focus in the ways you desire.

A light color palette, *left*, joins two adjacent spaces, emphasizing the open airiness of the architecture. Keeping the ceiling white draws the eye upward, giving a smaller room a great sense of loftiness.
Slate flooring, *above*, anchors a room that might have seemed adrift beneath soaring cathedral ceilings. The color and weight ground the space and draw the eye down to the furnishings' level. The contrast of the dark slate against the surrounding wood floor further defines the boundaries of the room.

Monochromatic displays, *below*, allow you to present collections while maintaining a spacious feeling. **Create a focal point**, *bottom*, with a bold orange sofa. The vibrant color makes the piece appear to come forward, and its low-slung design balances the vertical lines of the wall of built-in shelving. **This napping and reading nook**, *right*, enjoys an abundance of light and air near patio doors. Mirrors are great space expanders and can seem to add a window to a small space.

color

Choosing color is almost always more of an emotional decision than a logical one. The way we feel about color is instinctive. It's the reaction we have to warm reds or cool blues, lights or darks, a lot of color or a little, that gives us a first impression of any space.

The best place to start with color in a living room is to ask yourself what mood you want to create in it: invigorating or soothing, intimate or inviting. Your answer may lead you to paint the walls in a tranquil shade of sky blue, or to make an exclamation with bold terra-cotta.

In general, the larger the surface area, the more saturated a color appears. If you're experimenting with strong color, try out those hues first in smaller or transitional spaces, like hallways or entryways. Be aware, too, that color can create spatial illusions. Deeper colors seem to draw walls and ceilings inward in a large room; lighter ones are expansive and hide architectural flaws, making a small space feel larger.

Colors will change depending on a room's illumination. Over the course of a day, the shifting quality of light can make colors take on different

Every color has its own personality. Look to the shades you already love – in clothes, in paintings, in nature – to find the ones you want to live with.

Explore the possibilities. There are no rules for selecting the colors that make you feel most at home. Begin with a neutral palette, then add color by way of furnishings and other accessories. This is a good way to test the look and feel of a color scheme in your space. Let that embolden you to try out more dramatic hues; if you still want more color, break out the paintbrushes.

Designers often approach color palette choice with a strategy for an entire house. Choosing colors that are related in temperature, family, or tone for adjoining or surrounding rooms ensures that the views in an enfilade – rooms connnected in succession – will be attractive and harmonious.

casts. Bright midday light can fade colors that look fuller in the morning. The pink flush of a sunset can add shadings even to pure white rooms. At night, electric lighting adds its effect, and the hue and transparency of lamp shades also affect color. With all these variables, it's important to test paint colors by painting swatches on a wall and viewing them at different times of day. This isn't just something designers do; it's essential for getting precisely the color you want.

The most important thing is to trust your feelings. Colors that are in fashion or favored by "experts" won't suit your home if they don't speak to your heart. Choose colors you love.

Living with Color

A bolder-than-expected wall color wakes up the decor of a room
steeped in tradition. Choose a hue that's warm to enhance the dark
tones of wood and leather; keep it bright to add verve. The result:
a fresh take on modern nostalgia, an inspired fusion of old and new.

A room whose walls are washed in yellow seems steeped
in sunlight. Used daringly on all four walls or just on one,
yellow hues from pale butter to bold marigold quite simply
add energy. Colors with intense pigmentation seem to
advance toward the viewer, so these hues are perceived
as vibrant. Strong color helps to highlight everything it
surrounds. Yellow, especially in its primary form, feels
pure and uncomplicated – it makes a great foil for
traditional, dark-hued wood or leather furniture.

If your taste leans toward classic furniture, a strong wall
color can make the difference between a simply elegant
room and a stunning one. Painting your living room a
bold color is one way to express a modern, adventurous
spirit while still using traditional or heirloom furniture
or maintaining a period style.

More sumptuous than cream or ivory, yellow shares their
warmth but takes it up a notch, and brings out the natural
honey tones in almost any wood. Here, dark accents like
the black table and plush pillows emphasize the vitality of
the yellow, like a black mat surrounding a colorful photo.

A painting of a horse, *left*, suits the room's clubby ambience; set against a
crisp backdrop with a pair of lamps, it adds a dash of wry humor. **A collection
in creams and ivories**, *right*, harmonizes with the warm tones of the room;
darker furniture stands out against the wall color.

In this room, bright yellow serves as a bold "neutral." Neutrals don't need to be pale; they simply have to dominate visual territory and serve as a backdrop. Used in this way, many colors can work as neutrals.

White painted trim draws out the room's architectural lines, while the palette of warm browns and rusts provides a feeling of intimacy. Minimalist touches, like choosing simple pillows and using a coir area rug instead of a formal carpet, keep the space modern. The enduring style of the leather furniture creates a bridge between old and new.

Antique clocks, *above*, march up the stairs, establishing this room's time-oriented theme. **A retro telephone**, *right*, atop a watchmaker's cabinet, gives one club chair a vintage look; a contemporary geometric blanket drapes the other. A stellar bench serves as a pedestal for a sculptural display of large, timeworn clock hands.

Color Palette

The brilliance of marigold yellow against brown and black neutrals brings this room to life, updating it with a modern attitude. Warm and vibrant marigold walls brighten rooms that receive little light. The more light the room gets, however, the warmer the marigold tones appear. Black furniture and accessories help delineate the space, and brown leather upholstery grounds the room. Bright accents of color in the modern, geometric blanket draped over a chair arm contrast with the room's neutral palette.

Bringing color to a living room can make vintage furniture or styles suddenly seem current. The vitality of a new color can also prompt you to play up the contrast with other vintage pieces. This at-home bar celebrates the resurgence of cocktail culture, while leather club chairs recall 1930s Parisian nightclubs. The vibrant yellow backdrop lends a modern twist to the classic setup.

Materials

Leather Made from tanned animal hides, leather is one of nature's most durable materials. Used to upholster living room furniture, high-quality leather gets softer and more beautiful as it ages. Black and brown are classic leather colors, but manufacturers now dye leathers in a range of hues.

Velvet Traditionally woven from silk, cotton, or wool, velvet has a raised pile, which consists of rows of loops that are cut to produce a fur-like texture. Velvet, which has been used for draperies since the Middle Ages, adds an elegant texture to furnishings. How well a velvet resists flattening depends on its yarn quality and pile density.

Painted wood Painting wood furniture adds color, texture, and attitude. Distressed woods have a more casual presence; glossy finishes are more formal.

A black console and vintage bar, *left*, combines black with silver tones, which look sharp and graphic against a sunny hue. The lamp is fashioned from an old seltzer bottle. **A quilted velvet seat cover**, *above*, adds a diamond-patterned textural twist to the sofa and makes it a more inviting surface for napping. Covers like these can be easily sewn to cover worn cushions.

Warm up a room with red, *this page.* Provide a dramatic backdrop for furnishings with this rich, lacquered hue. Long associated with wealth and luxury, red was once the favored wall color for picture galleries because it was thought to enhance the paintings. Here, it seems to draw the walls closer, creating a warm, cozy atmosphere that accentuates the brown leather and the jewel tones of the silk drapery, throw, and pillow.

How to Balance Color

Color is to a room what rhythm is to music: it sets a mood and emotional temperature. Here, a corner of a room changes mood with different combinations. In general, warm colors (reds and yellows) convey a rich, cozy feel; cooler ones (blues and violets) are relaxing. Experiment with colors to find the balance you like. If a palette feels too warm, cool it with white. If a space feels too cool, spice it up with reds or yellows.

This nuanced rose color, *left*, is predominantly warm, but has underlying cool tones that resonate with the purple and white dupioni silk pillows and the white linen chair. **Pair deep blue walls**, *below left*, with white trim for a strong, graphic, yet classical effect. **Create a calm space**, *below*, with pale lavender walls. Add a leather chair and a smocked velvet pillow to provide a visual counterpoint and subtle contrast.

How to Accessorize with Color

Bringing color into the living room can be done in a variety of ways. Of course you can cover the walls, ceiling, or even the floor with a coat of paint. Or, you can simply dot the room with colorful fabrics, accessories, and botanicals; this is a great way to brighten up a room or change its look over time. Different window treatments and rugs can change the overall perception of color in a room, even if the wall color remains the same. Sometimes it's best to pick just one or two places in the room to highlight color, creating brilliant focal points and allowing the rest of the space to remain neutral. That way, you ensure that the color will have impact.

Jewel-toned pillows and drapes, *above*, add splashes of color to a beige sofa and are easily changed with season or whim. **Ceramic pomegranates**, *top right*, on a stone platter add sophisticated seasonal color to a room. **Brightly colored wheels of fortune**, *right*, complement a vivid red leather chair and create a strong focal point.

High-contrast color combinations, *left*, emphasize the outlines of furnishings and accessories, and they need not be limited to black and white. This classic pairing of Wedgwood blue and white gets an update with a blue-green cabbage plant set in the fireplace and a deep red oxalis on a side table next to the mantel. **Bells of Ireland set into bowls**, *below left*, are an impromptu alternative to a traditional flower arrangement. **Lustrous blue and green pillows**, *below*, perk up a lichen-colored velvet sofa. Shiny fabrics like dupioni silk are often best used as accents to offset a matte surface.

Warm wall colors

A living space decorated with a palette of warm colors – wheat, wine, and gold, for example – has a welcoming atmosphere that makes people want to linger. We've selected a sampling of warm wall colors ideally suited to living rooms. To balance saturated warm colors like cranberry or rich plum, use a few pale neutrals like ecru or almond to keep the space feeling airy and alive. All color families include hues, midtones, and deeply saturated colors. To create visual interest, mix up the tonal quality of the warm colors you choose.

Neutral wall colors

Our sampling of neutral wall colors coordinates with hues both cool and warm. Even so, cool neutrals like grays and whites are generally the best match for blues, violets, and greens. Warm neutrals like creams and taupes pair well with tones of red and yellow.

Cool wall colors

Cool colors – those predominantly in the blue and green ranges – can be pale or saturated, subtle or active. Our sample options of cool wall colors for the living room can all make a space feel fresh and restful. Suggestive of sea and sky, cool colors can make a living room seem more spacious and airy. They're also great for providing respite in warm climates. To warm a room dominated by cool tones, try adding ivory or beige; for crisp contrast, paint the trim a pure, high-gloss white.

wall, furnishing, and accent colors for your living room

How to coordinate colors

We've created this guide to help you choose colors for furnishings and accessories. By using core or basic colors for foundation pieces and layering in coordinating accessories in basic or accent hues, you can easily create a sophisticated living room palette.

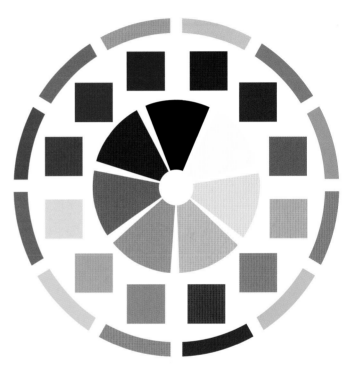

Core colors, shown in the middle, offer a foundation that coordinates with every range on the color wheel. Core hues are often the best choices for key pieces and larger furnishings. These neutrals can be used as a background or can comprise a simple, sophisticated palette on their own.

Basic colors, shown in the second ring, imbue a living room with richness. Basic colors are good choices both for larger furnishings and as accent tones in a core color–based palette. Hues in the basic color range mix easily with the core and accent tones within their family, or they can be accented with other colors.

Accent colors, shown in the wheel's outermost ring, are the fashion colors that can be added through accessories to enliven a palette of basic and core hues. If you're bolder, you can use these on larger pieces or on walls, but most people reserve stronger colors for smaller accents that can be changed seasonally.

texture

The soul of any room lies in the details, and every detail is clothed in a specific material. Smooth or rough, hard or soft, polished or distressed, texture makes a room visually unique and invites you to linger.

A captivating living room is one that's texturally engaging, whether it calls upon contrasts for drama (stone walls with silk drapes) or complements for harmony (glossy paint, sheer curtains, and waxed wood floors). Rough textures of wood or wicker, or fabrics like wool and linen, can transform a cool, open space into one that's

room special character. In the living room, bringing in rugs, carpets, and mats is the easiest way to make floors comfortably cushioned and visually lively. Whether shag, chenille, or kilim, sheared or looped, rugs provide a base layer of depth and complexity for a living room's textural palette.

Textiles of all kinds enrich a space, and a living room presents endless possibilities to showcase the beauty of fabrics. Pillows, throws, slipcovers, and drapes bring an entire tactile vocabulary to a living room, and are easy to change when the mood strikes you to update the room's atmosphere.

Texture is the most sensory element in a living room. Make every surface pleasing to the touch and the eye; choose luxurious fabrics, furnishings, and finishes.

alive with warmth; metal, glass, and high-sheen fabrics like silk bring fresh sophistication to a rustic space. Having mostly cool or mostly warm textures can set the atmosphere of a room.

When your goal is to add layers of texture, consider all the surfaces in the room. Look especially for ways to highlight the most physically and visually engaging parts of the space. If there are areas to which you'd like people to gravitate, use inviting textures to draw instant attention.

Floors are one of the largest surfaces you use in any room, so they have major textural impact. Whether you choose flagstone or wood, concrete or carpets, interesting floor textures can give a

Be strategic about how you incorporate texture into your space. In spring and summer, use flat, crisp materials like cotton, voile, and linen to keep a room feeling cool and comfortable. In fall and winter, bring in chunky blankets, plush rugs, and velvet, chenille, and faux-fur throws.

Surrounding yourself with the things that make you feel most at home ensures that you'll use your living room to its full potential. Let texture be an indulgence. Wrap up in a cashmere blanket for a decadent winter nap; fall into a jumble of quilted silk pillows on a sofa or daybed. Luxurious textures add comfort, color, and interest to any room, making it special for everyone who uses it.

A Natural Home for Texture

Elements from the outdoors, like stone, dried botanicals, and hewn wood, breathe life into a subdued, tonal space. Rough, unfinished materials stand out against smooth, polished surfaces, each complementing the other. Natural textures create offhand elegance.

One way to invite texture into a living room is to find the room's focus and use it as a starting point. Sometimes a fireplace, an interestingly shaped archway, or a window seat is a room's natural focal point. You can play off existing materials inherent in your home's architecture to create a canvas of textural possibilities, whether your room is clad in plaster or wood, metal or marble.

To add textural depth, employ the room's surfaces as well as its accessories. Weathered or distressed finishes steep a room in history, and mouldings and walls can contribute tactile richness as surely as draperies or upholstery.

Put to imaginative use, everyday materials can become provocative additions. Fill a bowl with crinkly kraft paper and place it on the hearth for handy kindling. Use thick jute to tie off white twill slipcovers, marrying rough with smooth. Create a sculptural paperweight with a handful of stones or a confetti of colored sea glass that evokes memories of last summer's walk on the beach. Even the simple choice of pillows and the way they're placed against furnishings can highlight the beauties of texture.

A soft sheepskin rug, *left*, contrasts with the rough surfaces of a limestone fireplace, crumpled kindling paper in a rusted metal basket, and bundles of twigs and sticks. **An old wire gathering basket**, *right*, is something you might pass without a glance at a flea market, but with a creative eye for texture, unexpected beauty can be found in the humblest of objects.

Take a cue from nature, where all is in harmony. Varied textures, especially those from outdoors, shape a soothing space and infuse it with interest.

Sometimes texture can suggest temperature: smooth and shiny textures give a cool impression; soft, raised textures convey a sense of warmth. Use these attributes to create different effects. Displays combining fabrics or finishes of very different temperatures can be visually engaging; using textures of similar temperatures brings a sense of quiet harmony to a room.

An aged pewter teapot and a stack of stones, *above*, make an appealing still life atop a stack of thickly textured cotton blankets. Soft fabrics, *right*, add visual texture, from the floor to the walls. Piles of pillows turn a daybed into an inviting nest for lounging. Sheer and opaque draperies soften the wall of windows and allow easy adjustment of light levels.

Design Details

Color Palette

A simple palette of white, powder blue, and palest green reflects the purity of winter. Cool, neutral colors evoke a contemplative feeling and create a calm atmosphere. The room's many tones of white and blue, from its sheepskin rug and canvas slipcovers to its pillows and artwork, create a spectral richness that doesn't distract from a multitude of textures. Beige adds a warm note in such natural accents as bundled twigs, kindling paper, and wooden stools.

Materials

Sheepskin Long used for furnishings, especially fireside rugs, plush white sheepskin combines lush softness with rugged resilience, and adds texture to any room.

Mahogany Deep-hued wood flooring brings a primitive exoticism to this space. While many tropical woods are endangered, several suppliers are now managing mahogany forests in more responsible ways. See Room Resources, page 183, for more information.

Limestone This room's French limestone mantel looks like it has existed for centuries, which is practically true: limestone is made from the mineral calcite, which comes from the beds of evaporated seas and lakes. Because limestone is softer than many stones, it crumbles gently over time, becoming more beautiful with age.

The bundles of twigs and branches in this room evoke the natural world and serve as earthy "bouquets." You can bring any season inside with items gathered from the local landscape. Look to the textures and colors of the outdoors when you choose fabrics, artworks, and accessories. In winter, a palette of blues, whites, and browns may feel most natural, while in summer you may gravitate more toward sunny yellows, greens, and tans.

A rough-hewn African Senufo stool, *above and left*, is carved from a single block of wood and holds handcrafted wooden objects. The repetition of wood throughout the room adds both visual and tactile appeal. **Another primitive stool**, *above*, holds ceramic objects, an island of smoother surfaces in a sea of deep texture.

How to Layer Soft Textures

Whether you're partial to luxurious fabrics like cashmere or velvet or to practical flat-weave textiles like linens and cottons, introduce a variety of textures and patterns throughout your room with pillows, throws, and draperies to create the most comforting environment possible. Consider durability and washability as you select the materials to fill your space, and strike a balance between aesthetic and functional concerns. Fortunately, some luxury fabrics like faux suede can be washable, giving you the best of both worlds. Finding fabrics that are appropriate to several seasons, such as silk, also makes good sense.

Rich chenille drapes create drama, *above*, lined with dupioni silk and tied back with gold tassels. **On the floor**, *top*, layer pleasingly plush textures such as lambswool with practical, durable ones like woven seagrass. **A matelassé throw**, *right*, is topstitched for pleasing texture; soft brushed twill has a diagonal weave that makes it durable.

Get comfortable, *left*, in a daybed piled high with texture, and make pillows central to your living room. Arrange fabrics in a beautiful collage that invites touch. Here, an exotic collection of textiles tops an Indian cotton throw: beaded blue silk, faux suede, tufted cotton, woven pandan (a natural leaf from Malaysia), and shibori-pleated silk. Shibori is a Japanese technique for dyeing and shaping fabric.

An elegant gray cashmere throw, *left*, is simply alluring draped over a leather Mies van der Rohe daybed. A handmade basket filled with smooth stones adds a pleasing juxtaposition of textures that complements the pared-down style. A textural medley, *above*, of fringed and embroidered tapestry pillows and a channel-stitched quilted silk throw make a sofa an ultra-chic perch.

Find Your Style A select guide to choosing and using the best

Soft flooring

As one of the largest surfaces in the room, the floor offers possibilities for instantly softening the look of a space. Layering carpets with rugs helps define discrete zones (an area for relaxing and a path for walking through the space, for example), lets you add a range of colors and patterns, and, most of all, creates a sense of warmth and intimacy in a living room.

Wool shag A tufted rug with long, twisted yarns, shag invites lounging and fills a room with softness.

Natural fiber mats Rugs made of coir, jute, seagrass, or sisal are relatively inexpensive, stain-resistant, and durable. Use them in high-traffic areas or to add natural texture to a room.

Flat-weave wool rugs Flat weaves resist dirt better than deep pile rugs and are soft, luxurious, and durable.

Soft furnishings

From plump sofas to easy chairs and ottomans, soft furnishings bring an essential level of comfort to a living room. Scatter-back sofas have loose pillows that beckon in casual fabrics such as twill and denim. Tight-back sofas have sleek backs without cushions that are tailor-made for leather and faux suede. Using textiles of varied textures fills a room with richness.

Cotton twill A tightly woven fabric characterized by a diagonal grain, twill is a durable textile. Denim, an identical weave, is traditionally dyed indigo.

Leather and suede Classic and sophisticated, leather and suede are tear and stain resistant; they grow more beautiful with age.

Velvet A soft, luxurious fabric with a rich sheen, velvet with extra-dense pile works well for upholstery.

Soft accessories

Pillows, throws, and other soft accessories encourage you to settle in and stay awhile. Choose colors and textures that complement your living room's existing furniture, upholstery, and slipcovers. Try pairing leather and faux fur, chenille and brushed twill, or cashmere and velvet. You can easily change soft accessories to add accents of color and texture to a room.

Faux fur Made of soft acrylic fibers, faux fur lends a luxurious touch. Available in many thicknesses and colors, its plush texture is irresistible.

Chenille French for "caterpillar," chenille is a loose, plush weave that is both warm and lightweight. Its yarn gives it a light sheen.

Faux suede A strong, silky-soft microfiber that feels like real suede, faux suede is machine washable.

soft and hard textures for your living room

Hard flooring

Easy to clean and long-lasting, hard flooring is a perfect foundation for living rooms. Wood floors are warm; tile floors offer many color and pattern options; stone floors are classic and long-wearing. Whether solid or patterned, wide-board or narrow, choose the material and style that best fits your living room's decor and suits the way you live.

Tile Heat-resistant and hardwearing, tile feels cool to the touch, so install radiant heat for added comfort.

Wood Warmer than tile, wood also absorbs vibration and sound. It's available in a variety of types, in strips, planks, parquet tiles, and laminate.

Stone The longest-wearing surfaces, marble, limestone, slate, and granite are popular living room options. As with tile, radiant heat is advised.

Hard furnishings

Hard furnishings lend solidity to a living room and offer many finish options: sleek and lacquered, natural and waxed, or stained and polished. Bring color into your decorative scheme with painted woods, or show off wood's natural qualities with simple varnishes and stains. Metal furnishings can be polished, sealed, distressed, or painted.

Natural or stained woods Warm-toned woods bring nature inside. Their grain and luster add both visual and physical texture to your space.

Painted wood Whether smooth or textured with distressed finishes, painted wood offers color versatility.

Metals Bronze, iron, and steel have a cooler look than wood. Finish options include reflective, matte, galvanized, painted, or even rusted.

Hard accessories

Whether glass, ceramic, or metal, hard accessories bring a strong sense of form to a space, in contrast to the room's soft accessories. Whether decorative or functional, displayed singly or in collections, sculptural accessories add texture, color, and a finishing touch to a living room's decor. They're also often the most personal accessories in a room.

Glass Because it reflects and refracts light, place glass displays near a window to make the most of changing light throughout the day.

Ceramics Whether glazed or unglazed, matte or shiny, ceramics' textures suggest a handwrought quality.

Metal The many colors of metal can subtly affect the way a room feels. Gold, bronze, and brass add warmth; silver, chrome, and pewter are cool.

furnishings

Furnishing a living room is like filling a wardrobe with things you might wear every day. As with clothing, basics come first. When selecting main furniture pieces (sofas, chairs, armoires, and side and coffee tables), classics are always best. Start with a generously proportioned sofa (as versatile as a favorite black sweater). Add a comfortable armchair or leather club chair (the equivalent of a well-made suit). Once you have easy-to-live-with foundation pieces, you can begin to dress up your room with details that add personality, intrigue, and interest.

When choosing furniture, keep the proportions of your space in mind. Oversized furniture in a small room can be overpowering and could compromise traffic flow, while pieces that are too small produce an environment where the space, rather than the people in it, dominates. Create a sense of balance by choosing furniture that is the right size, shape, and scale for the room.

Dissimilar pieces can be visually linked by grouping them closely together, or by relating them to a common line, such as along a wall or the edge of a rug. You can also arrange furniture

Furnishing with comfort and flair is simple: use furniture that has good lines and bold shapes; add unique pieces and heirlooms for wit and soul.

Furnishing is also about considering the room's most beautiful elements and deciding how you would like the space to flow. Is there a fireplace you'd like to be near while nestled on the sofa, or a window with a great view that you want to call attention to? Choose pieces that you can arrange to take advantage of your room's assets.

Most people design their living rooms with a combination of a sofa and comfy armchairs, but that's just one option. If you have space, try using a pair of sofas facing one another, or just gather a few club chairs informally around a coffee table. Add a loveseat, double-chair, or chaise longue, for curling up with a child to read a favorite story.

in relation to a backdrop – a large painting or an archway or other architectural element. Think of groupings of furniture as islands you can occupy for different purposes: socializing, watching TV, playing with children, or writing letters.

You can group pieces in your room symmetrically, asymmetrically, on the diagonal, or radiating out from a specific point, to create different effects. By finding core pieces that work in many orientations, you're free to reinvent the room later without entirely starting over. Shapely basics that adapt easily are the best building blocks to accomplish this. They'll see you through many years, rearrangements, and changing style trends.

Vacation-Style Comfort

R O O M   T O U R

Vacation homes put comfort first. They're furnished with character and a casual touch: low-key furniture, easy-to-sink-into seating, livable, washable fabrics. Adopt the same approach to make your living room an everyday retreat. It's a weekend look you can enjoy all week long.

The very things that make vacation time precious – breaking out of routines, escaping the phone and computer, focusing more on family – can inspire any living room's design. Consider what you love most about time away and bring it home to create a wonderfully relaxed atmosphere.

To give your living room a getaway feel, opt for the flexibility of an open-plan design, with discrete spots for dining, entertaining, relaxing, and reading. Zoning the space to carve out areas within one large room also lets you incorporate a variety of furniture. Choose pieces that have been used and loved, to give the room a sense of history. Recover or slipcover a beloved old sofa; give a set of vintage chairs pride of place around a central table.

Begin with generous sofas, and then focus on the rest of the room. Stack an oversized daybed with pillows and time-softened quilts. Have books, magazines, CDs, games, and bowls of snacks at hand. Choose a long dining table that invites everyone to pull up a chair. Revel in a style that makes everyone feel at home, and give your living room an atmosphere that has the comfortable familiarity of a favorite pair of faded blue jeans.

Sprawl in a sunbeam, *left*, or cozy up with a favorite book: every living room ought to incorporate a comfortable lounging space – or several. Make your living room adaptable by integrating plenty of areas to read, create, rest, and entertain. **Whimsical collectibles**, *right*, give a space a personal touch.

In a multipurpose living room, flexibility is the key to comfort. Design the space with furniture that offers lots of options: add a chair or two from the dining area when guests arrive; pull up an ottoman for an intimate chat – or place a few side-by-side to serve as a coffee table. An upholstered corner daybed can accommodate overnight guests as well as provide a reading nook. To bring a lofty space down to earth, choose colors and styles that ground the room. Here, a red and blue theme mixed with earth tones unifies the space, yet allows each area to embody a look and feel of its own.

Line up a collection of glass bottles, *above,* to create an offbeat centerpiece that runs the length of the table. **A long rag-rug runner,** *right,* divides this large room lengthwise. Runners or rugs can help visually demarcate areas that have been designed for different uses.

Turned back-to-back in a spacious corner, two entryway benches create an impromptu mudroom, where family and guests can leave their coats, boat gear, skis, and muddy boots (acid-stained cement floors like these stand up well to heavy traffic). Arranged in this way, the benches appear less formal than they would if placed against a wall, and offer an innovative way to divide the space. Although they are simple, sturdy pieces, the benches have good lines and shapes. They perfectly express the room's casual style.

An array of mismatched wooden chairs, *left*, can be moved around the living room whenever seating is needed. **Storing muddy boots on a child's red wagon**, *above*, allows you to wheel them out to hose them off. **A hardworking mudroom**, *right*, is created out of a corner and keeps gear handy for outdoor activities.

Design Details

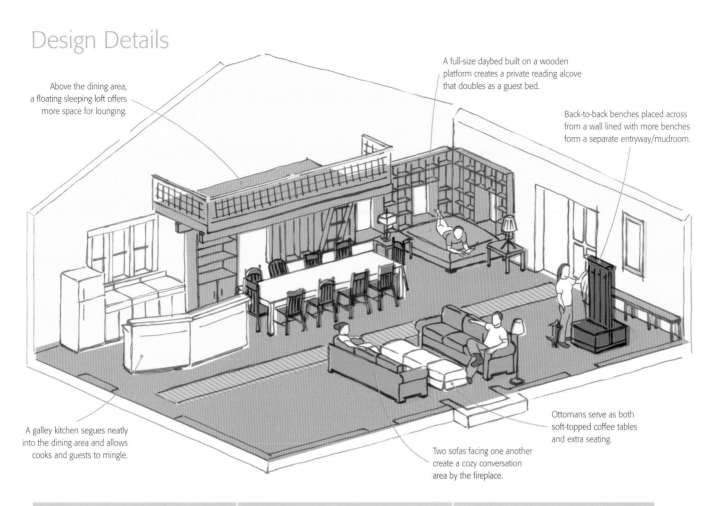

Above the dining area, a floating sleeping loft offers more space for lounging.

A full-size daybed built on a wooden platform creates a private reading alcove that doubles as a guest bed.

Back-to-back benches placed across from a wall lined with more benches form a separate entryway/mudroom.

A galley kitchen segues neatly into the dining area and allows cooks and guests to mingle.

Two sofas facing one another create a cozy conversation area by the fireplace.

Ottomans serve as both soft-topped coffee tables and extra seating.

Color Palette

Beige walls combined with red, white, and blue accents and upholstery produce a warming take on America's signature color scheme. This palette is perfect for a room featuring early American artifacts, Shaker influences, and a casual style. The surrounding tones of building materials extend and deepen the palette: an acid-stained cement floor, a redwood mantel, and a rust-colored plaster fireplace surround.

Room Plan

Divided into four zones – a dining area, a reading nook, a living room, and an entryway/mudroom – this large living space offers ample room for simultaneous activities. A long rag-rug runner divides the space lengthwise for efficient zoning, but the room still works as a communal area. A collection of casually mismatched dining chairs, which can be turned around to face the sofas, makes the space even more versatile. Ottomans can serve as coffee tables or can be pulled out to provide additional seating when needed.

Materials

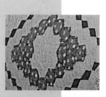

Quilts Stitching two layers of cloth filled with padding is an American art form. Here quilted cotton forms a colorful geometric pattern.

Concrete Cement, sand, gravel, and water form this strong flooring material. It can also integrate color and is easy to maintain.

Denim This sturdy cotton twill is a great washable slipcover option for casual living rooms, especially where kids and pets play.

Grouping pieces together in an L-shaped plan, *this page,* captures the look of sectional furniture and creates an intimacy that encourages conversation around the fireplace in fall and winter. Because the furniture is placed close together, this arrangement feels as cozy for two guests as it does for six. **This U-shaped grouping**, *opposite top,* takes a more formal approach, with chairs placed symmetrically across from each other and more space between the seating, for easy traffic flow.

How to Arrange Furniture

To achieve flexibility in your room, it's best to have pieces that easily adapt to different orientations. Look for multi-use furniture like a large ottoman or bench that can also serve as a coffee table. Changing slipcovers on sofas and armchairs, rearranging furniture, and using new accent pieces are all quick ways to adapt your rooms to changing functions and seasons. This room relies on different arrangements for winter and summer, shifting the focal point from the fireplace to the garden.

When spring arrives, *below left*, orient the sofa toward the garden rather than the fireplace. Here, a lighter, airier coffee table, complemented by striped ticking pillows, suits the mood of the warmer months. **A diagonal arrangement**, *below*, makes a square space seem more dynamic. This configuration also capitalizes on the window view, an enticing option in summer when the garden is in full bloom.

How to Reinvent a Side Table

Furniture and objects can have more than one useful life. Pieces that you love can occupy different spaces and can serve different purposes as time goes by. Take side tables, for example. Essentially, all you need is a flat surface next to your sofa or armchair 17–28 inches above the floor, with space enough for some combination of lamps, books, drinks, and decorative objects. Think beyond the ordinary. A milk pail, a wooden chest, a trunk passed down through generations, or a tall stack of books could serve your needs equally well and can add an unexpected personal touch to your room's decor.

A clean-lined, round wooden table, *opposite far left*, is a chairside classic and an elegant statement in simple surroundings. **Repurposed table options**, *opposite top to bottom,* include an old butter churn, a small antique desk, and a well-worn kitchen step stool. All give a room a personal touch. Think about color, texture, and shape when considering repurposed objects, which can have an appealing sculptural quality.

A metal bistro table, *left*, though designed for patio use, brings a bit of the garden into this living room and contributes to its casual style. **A shining mirror inlay**, *above*, spruces up a low wooden table. The mirror plays with light and adds interesting reflections to the room. Resurfacing a favorite table with clear glass laid over a collection of family photos, postcards, or dried flowers is an inventive way to bring new life to a worn piece and at the same time preserve a collection.

How to Dress a Sofa

Use throws and pillows in different textures and colors to transform your sofa. Changing a sofa's soft accessories is a quick and easy way to change the whole atmosphere of a living room. Warm up the room for winter with heavier textures and deeper hues; lighten it for spring with crisp linens and a refreshing blend of brightly colored pillows. Fabrics in neutral colors can work year-round; whites and creams can be dressed up or down in almost any surrounding. Mix the sizes, materials, and shapes of pillows and throws to reinvent the look of your living room as the mood strikes you.

For a lush look with lots of texture, *opposite page*, mix smocked velvet pillows with quilted ones, add a small beaded accent pillow, and set them all against a tweedy chenille throw. Dramatic colors match the rich fabrics and patterns for a dressier look.

Fashion a peaceful reading spot, *top*, with plush knit and tapestry pillows of different sizes alongside quilted satin, in both a pillow and a channel-stitch quilt. The closely related colors keep the look balanced; satin adds romance.

A soft wool blanket, *center*, draped over a sofa's center leads to an unexpected symmetry between tufted heathered wool pillows and stacked velvet ones. A dash of bright red adds presence. This is contemporary style with a twist.

Leather and faux-fur pillows, *bottom*, create an ultra-chic effect. Oblong pillows on the sides serve as impromptu armrests. With two very strong materials, no further embellishment is needed. The faux-fur throw here reinforces the look and further softens it.

lighting

Good lighting enables activity, enhances color, and – most importantly – gives a room a sense of warmth and life. Light fixtures also bring fun and fashion to a space. Use lighting in practical and provocative ways to alter the mood in your living room.

One of the keys to creating a comfortable and flexible room is to layer the lighting. Use a mix of ambient, task, and accent lighting to delineate different zones. Establish a plan that allows you to adjust the room's illumination levels gradually from bright to dim to suit your needs.

Task lighting is typically provided by table or floor lamps, recessed can lights, or a combination of the two. Task lights are the most versatile in a lighting plan, because you can rearrange them or change their look with a quick switch of shades. It's important to keep the contrast low between levels of general and task light, both for a pleasing balance and to avoid eyestrain.

Accent lights bring flashes of personality to a living room. Adjustable spotlights, either on tracks or recessed into the ceiling, focus narrow beams on specific details you want to emphasize.

Lighting creates ambience and makes a space welcoming. Give each part of the room a flattering glow to celebrate moments grand and small.

Begin with the ambient, or general, layer; this is the light that simply makes the room visible. Next, consider the task lights you'll need for you and your family to read, work, or play. Add an accent layer – fixtures that focus on objects or architectural features you want to highlight or light sources that create specific moods.

Ambient lighting in a living room is especially important because the room is often occupied by more than one person. Whether it's from sunlit windows or skylights during the day or from flush, recessed, or hanging ceiling fixtures at night, ambient light offers the broad wash of diffused illumination required for soft, general lighting.

Picture and bookcase lights call attention to displays and create interesting focal points. Candles, tinted light sources, or novelty lights like those used during the holidays add romance and a festive sense of flickering movement.

Take into account that incandescent, fluorescent, and halogen bulbs each offer a different quality and temperature of illumination. Because light interacts intimately with all other elements of design, choose bulbs that affect the colors and textures of your room in ways that best establish the mood you'd like. Think like a painter: by adjusting the light palette, you can change the whole appearance of your living room.

A Warm Reception

The best living-room lighting offers hospitality, encouraging friends and family to gather and settle in. In this room, accents of lustrous fabric, polished wood, and reflective glass keep light's dynamic spirit in motion, while candlelight adds a flickering, animated glow.

One of the most immediate ways to bring graciousness to a room is by implementing a well-designed lighting plan. Humans are by nature drawn to light and attracted to whatever part of a room offers a beacon. By providing multiple sources – both an inviting wash of ambient light and a variety of task and accent lights – you establish the living room as a place where all will feel at home.

Individual lamps create an intimate feeling. Commonly used as sources for task-specific lighting, floor, table, and wall lamps – and their shades – can transform the mood of a room. Think of lamp shades as fashion accessories. They're easily updated when it's time for a change, either seasonally or for a fresh look. Translucent shades, such as those made of natural parchment, silk, handmade paper, or linen, softly diffuse light; opaque and semi-opaque shades alter the direction of light and focus the beam up or down.

Candles are not just for romance. They are infinitely useful for adding drama, warmth, and sparkle to a space. Place them here and there to form small pools of illumination on different surfaces throughout a room. Aromatic candles infuse a space with long-lasting scent.

A string of holiday lights, *left,* woven through dried twigs keeps a fireplace flickering year-round. An accent spotlight draws focus to a modern painting. **A cluster of candles,** *right,* illuminates fiery orange chrysanthemum blossoms and creates a festive moment in this dressed-for-entertaining living room.

Candles are for more
than special occasions.
Use them every day to
effect a gentle transition
to dusk, or to contribute
subtle color and scent.

Even small details can make a big
difference when it comes to lighting.
Whether you cluster votive candles
or glaze a brightly painted wall with
angled downlights to give it presence,
lighting draws attention wherever it
is focused. Emphasize furniture with
light: enliven a corner table with an
eye-catching lamp, or accent built-in
shelves with low-voltage halogen
bookcase lights. Backlight a sofa
with candles and a table lamp to
create subtle elegance (combining
backlighting with a reading light
also reduces glare).

You can fashion lamp bases from
anything: a treasured vase, primitive
pottery, even a shapely sculpture.
Use cherished heirlooms or quirky
collectibles to make lighting choices
that are purposeful and individual.

A floor lamp and a table lamp flank a sofa
and offer ample task lighting for reading or
conversation. The reflective surfaces of mirror
and glass add to the room's vibrancy. Tapers lend
geniality to this comfortable living room; stored
casually in a bowl, they don't even have to be
lit to produce a warming effect.

Design Details

A wall-mounted spotlight draws attention to the modern painting over the mantel.

Recessed ceiling fixtures fill the room with a wash of ambient light. Mirrored armoire doors amplify the room's illumination.

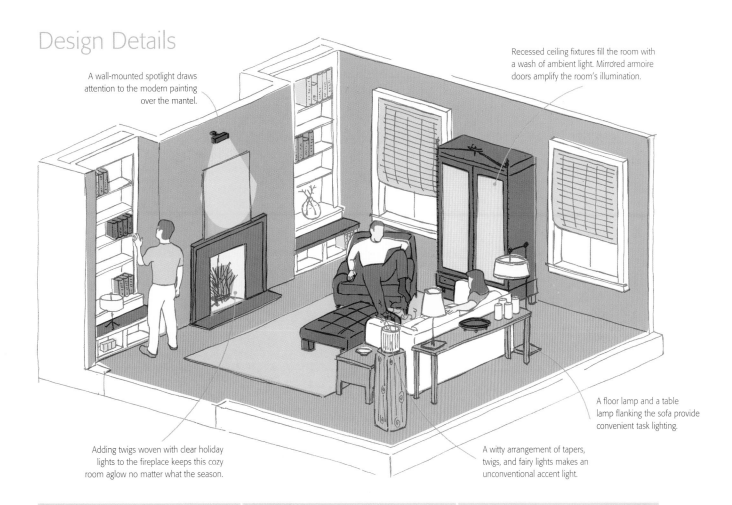

Adding twigs woven with clear holiday lights to the fireplace keeps this cozy room aglow no matter what the season.

A witty arrangement of tapers, twigs, and fairy lights makes an unconventional accent light.

A floor lamp and a table lamp flanking the sofa provide convenient task lighting.

Color Palette

Mushroom walls, cream twill upholstery, and caramel leather furniture create a warm, rich palette that works well with natural materials like bamboo and wood. The colors have an amber base that's enhanced by warm light, giving the whole living area a golden glow. Red accents contrast with the muted colors. The flat color planes of the wall, sofa, and ottoman have an abstract force that fits the modern setting.

Room Plan

Orienting the seating area to face the mantel communicates that this room is all about fire's warming glow. Dotting candles and accent lights around the room — behind the sofa, on a wooden-beam pedestal by the window, and in the fireplace — keeps the room feeling lively. Mirrored armoire doors make the room seem larger and more animated than it might otherwise; the mirrors and glass accessories amplify ambient light. A floor lamp and a table lamp flank the sofa, providing convenient task lighting.

Materials

Oriental rugs Traditionally from countries such as China, India, Iran, and Turkey, these richly patterned rugs are usually hand-knotted and can last for generations.

Mirrors The most common type of mirror is made of plate glass coated on one side with metal or some other reflective surface.

Bamboo Matchstick blinds, crafted from this woody, hollow-stemmed grass, filter natural light into a room.

How to Create Mood with Lighting

Gather family and friends with the welcoming radiance of warm light. Whether you're working with electric lights and shades or firelight and candles, there's no better way to shift the mood of your room than with lighting. Create a cozy mood for relaxing with a chairside lamp that casts a pool of light over the pages of your book, set a party mood with accent lights and mellow lamplight, or inspire romance with glowing firelight and votives. And don't overlook the impact of lamp shades. Not only are they an easy way to update a lamp's – and a room's – look, they can also change the color of lamp light, adding another layer of contrast or depth to a room's lighting scheme.

A shade fringed with beads, *top*, gives sparkle to a comfortable spot. **A gleaming metal samovar urn**, *above*, is wired to make an unusual lamp that presides over a corner reading table. **Votive candles**, *right*, in clear glass cups, add elegance to a celebration. The table's burnished surface catches the low flames' glow; vases, champagne flutes, and a silver bucket amplify reflections.

A vintage grocer's scale, *top*, holding a group of candles becomes a casual chandelier; the differing heights of the pillars add style. **Create atmosphere around artwork**, *above*, with votives lined up along the front of a ledge. **A candlelit vase**, *above right*, nicely balances the beam of a shaded sconce, warming an all-white mantel display. **Clustered pillar candles**, *right*, make a family photo a focal point. Built-in shelving frames the scene.

Ambient lighting

Think of ambient lighting as your living room's overall light wash, whether it's sunlight streaming in through the windows during the day or overhead lights casting a warm glow through the room at night. Ambient light is the basic lighting layer, illuminating walls, open areas, and main pieces of furniture so that you can navigate the space with ease. Ambient light can be direct, bounced off a wall, or diffused through a shade to warm up the quality of the light. Dimmer switches allow you to modulate lighting to suit different moods and occasions.

Torchière

Task lighting

Designed to help you perform activities at close range, task lighting is a more location-specific layer of light than ambient lighting. Place wall sconces behind the sofa to facilitate reading, or use a swing-arm table lamp on a side or parson's table. Hang a pendant lamp low over a game table. Think about brightness, beam direction, proximity of the fixture to the task area, and the bulb's color temperature (its relative value of warmth or coolness) when selecting task-oriented lighting.

Table lamp

Accent lighting

Accent lighting provides dramatic spots of light wherever you want them and is the layer that allows you to change a room's mood and style most easily. Typically using narrow-beam lightbulbs, accent lights let you direct the eye to those objects or places in the room you find most visually appealing. Spotlight a favorite painting or sculpture on a wall or mantel, highlight a pleasingly textured wall with track lighting spots, or dot candles throughout the room to create a warm, natural glow.

Picture lights

ambient, task, and accent lighting for your living room

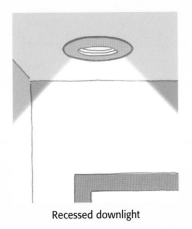

Recessed downlight

Pendant

Suspended uplight

Torchières are uplights that emit a soft, even wash of light.

Recessed downlights, or "can lights," are built into the ceiling and have a reflective lining.

Pendants hang from the ceiling. They come in different shapes and styles that can add another decorative element to a room.

Suspended uplights are ceiling-mounted fixtures that cast light upward and give an even glow.

Swing-arm lamp

Sconce

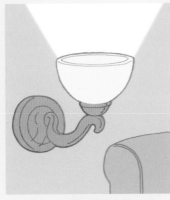

Floor lamp

Table lamps come in a variety of shapes, sizes, and wattages. For versatility, choose one that takes a three-way bulb.

Swing-arm lamps have adjustable arms that allow the light to be swung into position.

Sconces attach directly to the wall and can offer useful supplementary lighting.

Floor lamps are freestanding and may be adjustable in height.

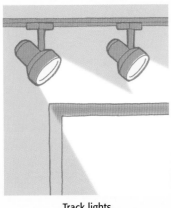

Track lights

Candles

Mini-chandelier

Picture lights perch over artwork to illuminate it. They are usually low wattage to minimize glare off reflective surfaces.

Track lights can be aimed to highlight architectural details and favorite objects.

Candles fill a room with warmth and animation; they can add color and scent as well.

Mini-chandeliers hang from the ceiling and add sparkle.

windows

Window treatments help to define the decor of a room. They can be sheer or opaque, light or heavy, classic or casual. As with the pleats and folds of a beautifully draped garment, you can tailor almost any kind of dressing to your windows, to stand out on its own or to reinforce the room's style.

Draperies, shades, blinds, and shutters can produce a clean, neutral backdrop or provide a full-dressed flourish. In either case, the way you choose to treat your windows lends rhythm to a room, adding pattern and color, light and shadow.

You might want to pick up a color of the season to echo flowers blooming in your garden. During cold months, create a cozier or more elaborate treatment with lush fabrics in warm or metallic hues. Heavier fabrics help retain heat, and deeper colors offer respite from winter's cold palette.

With interesting details around your windows like mouldings, beadboard, or brick, you can think of the inner layer as a tonal extension of the wall and keep it simply neutral. Or, you may want to draw more focus; plain walls may benefit from treatments that create graphic interest.

Window treatments are a visual filter between indoors and out. Let light come streaming in, or create a shelter with a soft wall of texture and color.

The first step in determining which treatment is appropriate for you is to simply live with your windows for a while. Notice where the light falls, and think about how you use the room. If you decide to dress your windows (and some are best left undressed for architectural interest or to maximize great views), consider using double-rod draperies. That way you can have both a basic, year-round layer closest to the window, and a second, outer layer that can be changed easily with the seasons. In spring and summer, a light outer layer lets you open the windows to feel the breeze; materials are generally solid and subtle, in simple weaves like linen and cotton.

Think about how you would like your window treatments to feel and function before choosing type, color, material, and style. Heavily draped, opaque window treatments tend to be more static and sculptural. Lighter or transparent ones have more movement and seem more casual.

Never underestimate the importance of hardware. Decorative rods, finials, holdbacks, and ties are the jewelry that lends elegance or whimsy to your windows. Using garlands of beads, colorful ribbons, or silk scarves as tiebacks can add a creative touch to your windows for the holidays or for celebrations. Fortunately, with window treatments, the options are nearly limitless.

Summer Sun, Winter Warmth

Just as you don warm garments in winter and shed them in spring, windows can be dressed lightly or heavily according to the season. Here, filmy voiles and lightweight linens cool off a summer living room; chenille and silk warm it back up for winter.

You can change the mood of a room from breezy to sheltered merely by changing window treatments and their accessories. Here, styling one room both ways illustrates how a simple change of window materials can transform the sensibility of your entire space. For summer, windows want to be casual, to let in sun and air and take in the surrounding views. In winter, with light getting low and drafts coming through in cold climates, you may want drapery that's as comforting and insulating as a colorful, toasty quilt.

For summery windows, begin with a pure flow of fabric. Carefree cottons, linens, voiles, and organdy are translucent and soften windows, but they still let in plenty of daylight. Opt for smooth fabrics to keep rooms feeling fresh. Add natural greens and citrus yellows to set off crisp whites; all three colors enhance a sense of airiness.

To emphasize the shape of your windows, hang drapes so that mouldings show. Or, make modest windows appear grand by hanging drapes well above the window frame and letting them glide to the floor. Tradition suggests leaving an inch between the bottom of draperies and the floor, but if space allows, consider the stylist's trick of puddling drapes onto the floor like the sweep of a long gown.

An abundance of sheers, *left*, gathered and tacked informally, creates a casual style. **Arrangements of flowers and fruit**, *right*, in clear glass vases and an open birdcage welcome the warm season with a lively flourish.

Even simple windows can be stylish when properly dressed. Hang sheer window-width panels to diffuse light subtly (because pleating adds body to treatments, it also tends to filter out more of the sun's rays). Plain sheers softly filter light; patterned ones add texture and cast dappled shadows. Curtains unadorned by valances or other top-treatments offer a cleaner, more streamlined look.

Here, grosgrain ribbon accents are a deft and delicate touch. You might also use silk, raffia, or even a scarf as tiebacks – or gather the curtains and tie them at their centers.

Sheer panels, *left*, whether casually tacked or neatly tied with ribbons, offer privacy without sacrificing light. **Seasonal flowers**, *above*, picked from the garden, enhance the summery palette. **Crisp white window treatments**, *right*, capture the light, warm-weather spirit along with pristine cotton, linen, and lace accessories.

Winter window treatments tend to be heavier and more formal than summer ones. Taffeta, damask, chenille, silk, and velvet are some traditional fabric choices. Pull them back with a tassel for a dressed-up look, and use lined drapery for a firmer structure and to better insulate the room from the cold. For drama and an element of surprise, try dense, matte-finished outer drapes contrasted with a luxurious, reflective inner lining. You can achieve this look by hanging contrasting drapes on a double rod or simply by stitching two drapes of the same size together.

The right window treatments give a room polish. Draperies, curtains, and shades can articulate a focal wall with an expanse of color, or emphasize the line of trim and mouldings. A floor-length column of drapes can elongate windows and lift attention to the ceiling. Be creative. Accessories like ties and holdbacks give drapes a more finished presence; try a gold belt or an antique brooch as an alternative to a traditional tieback. Decorate drapes with beads, clusters of pinecones, or glossy holly leaves to celebrate the spirit of the season.

Wine-colored chenille drapes, *left*, are lined with gold dupioni silk panels and swept back with tassels in this winter-accessorized room. **Bring in silk and beaded pillows**, *right*, autumn-hued dried leaves, and winter berries to celebrate the cool-season sensibility.

Design Details

Color Palette

Fresh colors like pure white, lemon yellow, and spring green make this room feel light and airy for summer. Green, the color of new growth, is naturally rejuvenating and fresh. Yellow, the color of sunshine, is its natural complement. White walls showcase seasonal flowers and sheer fabrics in citrus tones. This garden palette evokes a cottage dressed for summer, where everything is about the outdoors. Translucent window treatments modulate but don't obscure the day's intense sunlight.

Color Palette

In winter, dress up your living room with luxurious colors and heavier textures to create a welcoming retreat. In this room, the adaptable backdrop of white walls highlights an interplay of gold and wine hues. Glamorous and strong on its own, wine harmonizes beautifully with deep gold. This warm combination appears especially regal in the window treatments: wine-colored chenille draperies are lined with gold dupioni silk and swept back with tasseled tiebacks. Pillows echo the dramatic tones.

Materials

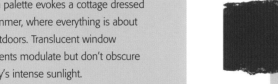

Voile A sheer fabric woven from cotton, silk, wool, or synthetic fibers, voile admits light yet moderates it. Voile curtains make a room feel light-infused but not sunbaked.

Twill This dense, tightly woven cotton is durable, washable, and relatively flat, making it a versatile weave for upholstery in both summer and winter seasons. Denim is an example of a twill weave.

Materials

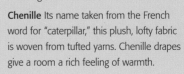

Dupioni silk Woven from two threads of the same or different colors, this fabric gives off a seductive sheen that contrasts elegantly with heavy chenille. Occasional meshing of filaments creates textural slubs.

Chenille Its name taken from the French word for "caterpillar," this plush, lofty fabric is woven from tufted yarns. Chenille drapes give a room a rich feeling of warmth.

How to Dress a Window

Windows are a key architectural element of any room; they literally frame your view of the world. The right window treatment can enhance a window's size, shape, and the way it filters light. Decide if you'd like a trim or wall mount (see page 118), and whether you'd like the curtains to pool dramatically on the floor or fall just below the sill. Choose materials that balance your need for privacy with your desire for light.

Sheer panels take on a romantic, billowy air, *opposite*: gather the bottoms at their midpoint and pin them up to the drape's center; a fabric tie finishes the look. **White cotton voile sheers,** *left*, are hung café style to lightly screen the window's lower half. **Rich dupioni silk drapes,** *below left*, are layered over whispery voile sheers for dramatic contrast. **Suede holdbacks,** *below*, are a stylish counterpoint to linen-cotton drapes. Mount holdbacks lower for a full and formal look.

Curtains and drapes

Window treatments affect the amount of light that a living room receives, frame its view, and hide or enhance the shape of its windows. Sheer fabrics like voile, organdy, and linen filter light and offer a casual look. Rich fabrics like velvet, silk, and chenille block light; their shapely folds look more formal. The style and material of the rod, and the way the drape attaches to it, also influence your window style.

Rods are usually mounted 4" above the window (A); to add visual height to a room, mount the rod even higher. Or, you can mount the rod at the top of the frame (B). To determine the length of drape that you need, measure the length of your window, deciding where you want the drape to fall: to the sill (from A or B to C); below the sill (from A or B to D); or 1" above the floor (from A or B to E), which allows for clearance. To pool drapes on the floor, add 6" to 8".

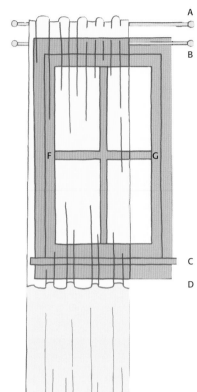

A **Rod** For *wall mount*: mount the curtain rod 4" above the window frame (A). For *trim mount*: mount the curtain rod at the top of the window frame (B). Extend the rod 1" to 3" on each side of the window frame as you please.

Width Measure the width of the window (F to G) and multiply that number by 1 for a tailored look, 1.5 for a standard look, or 3 for a full look.

C **Length** See the
D paragraph at left for instructions on measuring for length. When measuring, it's important to take into account the size of ring-tops, tie-tops, or other decorative tops, as they can add 1" or more to the length of a curtain or drapery panel.

Fabric panels

Fabric panels are easy, informal window treatments that can give a living room instant charm. They work equally well for light voiles and for heavier fabrics such as linen or canvas. Fabric panels can be tacked directly to a window frame, either in a looser, draped approach (*left*) or in a more formal, tailored fashion (*right*).

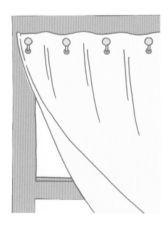

Tack the fabric directly to the window frame as shown.

Width Multiply the window width by 1 for a tailored look, 1.5 for a standard look, or 3 for a full look.

Length The panel can extend to the sill (B to C), below the sill (B to D), or to the floor (B to E).

drapery style for your living room windows

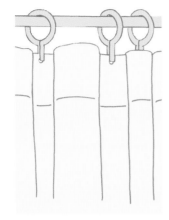

Rod To install ring-top or tie-top curtains or drapes, attach the curtain rod for wall mount (see the rod instructions at left). Extend the rod 3" to 4" on each side of the window, so the drapes can "stack back" to let in light. (Trim mounts are not well suited to this style, because light can show through the space between the rings.)

Ring-tops or tie-tops

This classic drapery and curtain treatment is wonderful for the living room because it allows window coverings to open and close with ease. Fullness suits this style: when measuring, multiply the window width by 3 and use two or more panels per side, as needed. Take the rings or ties into account when you measure for length, as they can add 1" or more to the top of the drapery panel.

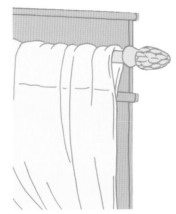

Rod To install pole-pocket curtains, mount the curtain rod for trim mount or for wall mount (see the rod instructions at left). Extend the rod 1" to 3" on each side of the window frame.

Width Measure the window width (F to G) and multiply by 3; use two or more curtain panels per side, as needed.

Pole-pocket rods

This style features a flat panel with a casing sewn at the top through which a rod can be inserted. Use ample fullness to allow the panel to shirr on the rod. Pole pockets are not as easy to slide along the rod as rings or tie-tops. However, most can be hung on drapery hooks, which attach to the pocket back and can be hung from rings. Decorative rod finials are a nice finishing touch.

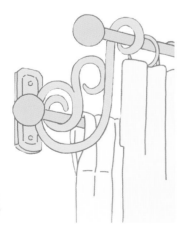

Rod To install a double rod, mount the inner, lower curtain rod 1" above the window frame and 4" beyond each edge of the frame. The outer rod will be several inches above.

Length Take into account the rods' varying heights when measuring for length. The drape can extend below the sill (A to D) or to floor (A to E).

Double rods

Multiply your options by installing a double rod. This lets you create a layered look with a sheer drape under a heavier drape. If the outer layer will be pulled back and the inner layer left as a screen for light, make the outer layer fuller to create drama when pulled back: when measuring, multiply the window width by 1.5 for a standard look (inner layer) or by 3 for a full look (outer layer).

storage

Storage is about more than managing the odds and ends of life. With thoughtful organization, it can also bring efficiency and style to everyday life. Conventional containers are handy, but they aren't the only storage options. Using a variety of furniture, repurposed pieces, boxes, and baskets, you can easily design a system that's as attractive as it is helpful.

Before you decide what to put things in, you must decide what to save. Embrace spring cleaning! Storage is first an editing process, so make sure that the things you have are actually being

Make storage your ally in helping you find things when and where you need them. Find opportunities throughout the room to integrate storage at every level: up high on shelves, in cabinets or armoires, down low along the floor, under the coffee table, or nested in side tables. Instead of putting containers where tradition dictates, place them where they naturally need to be (if the mail never makes it from the hallway basket to the desk, you need a new solution). Keep smaller items or multiples (keys, glasses, mail, magazines) in matched containers to maintain visual order.

Storage that's attractive and inventive is the key to clutter-free living. Choose solutions that complement your belongings and the way you use them.

put to use or are personally meaningful to you. Rearrange belongings as well as furnishings with the seasons to keep your room looking fresh. Finding the right place for everything becomes much easier when you have less to keep track of.

Next, consider how things will fit, where you'll want to find them, and how to fashion storage that caters to the items and your decor. Fitted containers that perfectly suit their contents are the ones you'll find most useful. But that doesn't mean resigning yourself to colorless boxes. Call on your ingenuity: use a favorite handbag to hold mail, dime-store candy racks to organize CDs, and Japanese bento boxes to catch loose change.

Whether your choices are functional or fanciful, new or old-fashioned, they can add style to your living room. Antiques and objects with history are intriguing and create moments of discovery. A flat-lidded steamer trunk provides both extra seating and toy storage; an antique pie safe might stow hats, mittens, and scarves by the front door.

Keep your own habits in mind when you choose storage solutions. The best ideas combine beauty with reality. A locked glass barrister's case may show off your books nicely, but it could also hinder your day-to-day enjoyment of them. No matter how attractive it looks, storage that doesn't work the way you do just doesn't work.

A Place for Everything

Smaller spaces demand resourceful storage solutions. In this intimate living room, ordinary items are called upon for unexpected new assignments. A solid wall of shelving does more than function as smart storage; it becomes a graphic backdrop to the entire room.

Everybody faces storage challenges, but the smaller the space, the larger those challenges. Well-conceived solutions for compact living rooms weave storage through the space, so it doesn't weigh down any one area.

In this house, a full wall of floor-to-ceiling shelves saves the day by stacking up storage and distributing it the full length of the room. Designed for the way people really live, the shelves readily mix a library of books, CDs, mementos, and everyday items and maintain clear organization. Colorful vintage food cans help sort bills and letters; spare change goes into an antique grocer's scale, which also acts as a clever bookend. The proximity of the shelves to the sofa allows them to stand in for side tables, further enhancing openness where space is limited.

Old-fashioned milk paint, a highly durable finish made of earth pigments, is used here on shelving to achieve a rustic look. Milk paint is widely available in many colors, and its matte finish makes it effective for eliciting a lived-in, country feel. In this room, the light paint also helps the large storage wall recede quietly into the background.

An antique grocer's scale, *left,* is a useful and creative addition to this bookshelf. Place favorite objects — even sturdy rocks — to divide subjects and give rhythm and balance to an arrangement of books. **Reserving shelf space for simple displays,** *right,* keeps the storage wall from seeming crowded.

The best storage is
simple, useful, and
welcoming: a low shelf,
a sturdy coat hook.

Entryways can almost always benefit
from more storage. By providing it at
many levels, you minimize the clutter
that often gathers in this high-traffic
area. Here, a console table makes
room for things on their way in and
out, so you don't have to rummage for
them. Its low shelf holds a vintage
suitcase where periodicals are stashed.

Bright patterned blankets, *left and right,* on the
low shelf of a console table are cinched tight with
leather belts, keeping them handy for use indoors
or to take out for picnics. **Storage meets display,**
above: an attractive Mexican coat hook becomes
a surprise picture hanger for a family photograph.
Storing off-season firewood in the fireplace,
right, adds color and texture in keeping with the
room's cast-earth hearth and rammed-earth walls.

A sofa pushed up against the wall of shelves creates an impromptu "attic" to store seasonal ornaments or less-frequently-used possessions. This arrangement provides hidden storage that's still accessible; it also opens up the center of the living space to make the room feel larger. A narrow caned bench serves as a coffee table and can be moved easily to serve as extra seating when guests arrive.

These shelves have been smartly designed to provide display as well as storage. Primitive bowls and baskets up high and a cluster of pillar candles mid-shelf are nicely framed by the shelving's open structure.

A full wall of shelving, *left*, needn't overpower a small room. Painting the shelves neutral tones and placing a sofa against them allows the storage to recede and form an attractive backdrop. **A travel souvenir**, *above*, is put to work as a witty book divider.

Color Palette

A palette of pale blue-green and earth tones is enlivened with the addition of burnt orange. The hues of the rammed-earth walls, cast-earth floor, and blue-green milk-painted shelves create a neutral backdrop that moderates the reddish orange kilim rug. With blue-green on the cool side of the spectrum and red-orange on the warm side, the earth tones hold the middle ground, bridging the two opposing colors. A warm-hued coffee table and cool white ceramics accent the palette on either side.

Materials

Milk paint A mix of casein (powdered milk protein), lime, and stable earth pigments, this all-natural paint adheres easily to porous surfaces such as wood. Milk paint's distinctive flat finish lends an authentic antique look even to new furnishings.

Rammed earth A mixture of earth, water, and cement is poured into molds and tamped down to create thick, highly compacted rammed-earth walls or floors. It is highly insulating and suitable for all climates. Cast earth, like the flooring here, is created by pouring an earth mixture into molds. It is not tamped, but instead is hardened by its calcined gypsum content.

Brushed twill This form of cotton is finished to emphasize the material's soft nap. Usually characterized by a diagonal weave, twill fabrics have a denser construction than identical plain weaves.

Storage for Everyone

A family room designed for working, playing, and relaxing carves out activity zones for everyone in the house. High or low, tucked away or in plain view, storage that's moveable and accessible ensures order and keeps a family running smoothly.

Today's family room is command central for the whole household. It's a place to work, play, socialize, and relax. Storage here must balance the need to keep items at hand with the desire to keep the room tidy and attractive. While many living rooms have a wall of built-in shelving to hold essentials, activities happen all around a family room, and storage options must follow suit. Zoning a room by function – alcoves for work, places for play, and a central multipurpose area – divides up the space for use by the entire family. Adding storage within each zone is a smart way to keep things neat yet nearby.

Storage can be hidden or out in the open. If your living room features plenty of visible storage in the form of bookcases, create subtle organization with a simple trick: keep it all white. Unified by a quiet color, storage containers (and the things they hold) tend to fade into the background. They also harmonize easily with white mouldings and with each other. White is a smart base color for storage that serves the whole family, because so many different items are available in white. It also works well with natural materials like rattan and wicker, and with most colors.

Choosing white supplies, *left*, keeps them visually quiet when they're stored among all-white shelving. **Places for toys and office supplies**, *right*, exist happily side-by-side. A dollhouse-shaped shelving unit helps encourage young children to put away their playthings.

Categorize, consolidate, and contain. Think like a product designer: start with the things you want to store, then match the container to them.

The best storage solutions take a realistic approach based on versatility and ease. Here, a paneled wall of closed media storage conceals wires and keeps electronics like the television and stereo out of sight when not in use. A coffee table's empty space is a handy framework for containers. Baskets work well because of their easy-to-grab handles, and their natural textures bring warmth to a room. Dedicating a storage basket to each member of the family makes it convenient to find or put away favorite items. Store essentials such as pencils and scissors in multiples to create a display that's useful as well as visually interesting.

Storage doesn't have to be square, *above.* Glass containers make items easy to spot and add color to the room. **A rough-hewn coffee table**, *right*, serves as a frame for wicker baskets tucked underneath and used as drawers to stow papers and books. The canister on top attractively keeps toy blocks together and embraces the family-friendly spirit of the room.

Design Details

Color Palette

Milky green, high-gloss white, and fire-engine red present a New England schoolroom motif that's perfect for a casual space suited to family living. Red and green are complements on the color wheel, meaning that they offset each other in temperature and strength. Primary red tempers the cool tones of the room and adds energy. Green, long associated with vitality and abundance, makes an uplifting background color. White on the painted ceiling and trim adds crisp, clean contrast.

Materials

Sisal Produced from the leaves of the agave plant, this strong, flexible fiber is woven into flat rugs with an even, highly textural surface. Machine-woven sisal rugs can be given a latex backing for increased durability and stain resistance. Sisal tends to hide dirt and absorb sound, making it a practical option for high-traffic areas.

Wicker Created with a technique of weaving bamboo, cane, rattan, or willow "weavers" around a coarser frame, wicker is used to make durable furnishings that can stand up to a century of normal use.

Cotton twill This variation of plain-weave fabrics makes durable, easy-to-wash slipcovers. Twill has a diagonal grain, giving it a slight texture that makes it more rugged than a plain weave. Denim is the identical weave, dyed indigo.

Stackable bins are a versatile solution for kids' items. Easily accessible to youngsters when in use, they free up floor space when stacked. And wheels on the bottom make them even handier: you can scoot them away when guests are expected. Chalkboard labels make bins easy to identify and change. Solutions like these help give children a sense of pride in their possessions and encourage them to put their things away so they won't be tripped over after playtime.

A vintage school desk, *left*, provides a nostalgic anchor to a child's corner of the room. Artworks can be added to the framed bulletin board's evolving collage. **Colorful pillows hung on hooks**, *above*, become a soft sculpture, keeping extras out of the way.

Transparent pantry jars, *top*, hold photographs and a matchbook collection. **Books stacked in baskets**, *above*, let you keep favorites close at hand yet moveable, freeing up room on shelves to store media or to display collections. **Exotically labeled food cans**, *above right*, organize letters and bills. **A carpenter's tool caddy**, *right*, makes a clever portable desk and allows you to settle down to work wherever you'd like.

How to Store with Style

Having a special place for the things you need most saves time. As with every aspect of design, you can approach creating storage with personal flair. Your senses of color and texture, style and materials – as well as your possessions themselves – will lead you to find storage options that look as good as the rest of your room. Inexpensive items like canning jars and tackle boxes can be just as useful as ordinary boxes, and are more visually interesting and dynamic. If an object catches your eye, think about its storage and decorative potential.

Built-in shelving, *left*, is a classic storage solution. Not only does it easily accommodate books, media, and decorative displays, it's also the most flexible of systems. Shelving can store all kinds of items in multiple ways, each of which allows easy access: in closed boxes (coded by color or type of container), on open shelves, or in baskets. All of these containers let you take out exactly what you need and return it to its proper place without moving other items around. **Storage gets dressed for style**, *above:* a sheer fabric scrim softens a wall of books without compromising accessibility; decorative items are interspersed for dramatic effect.

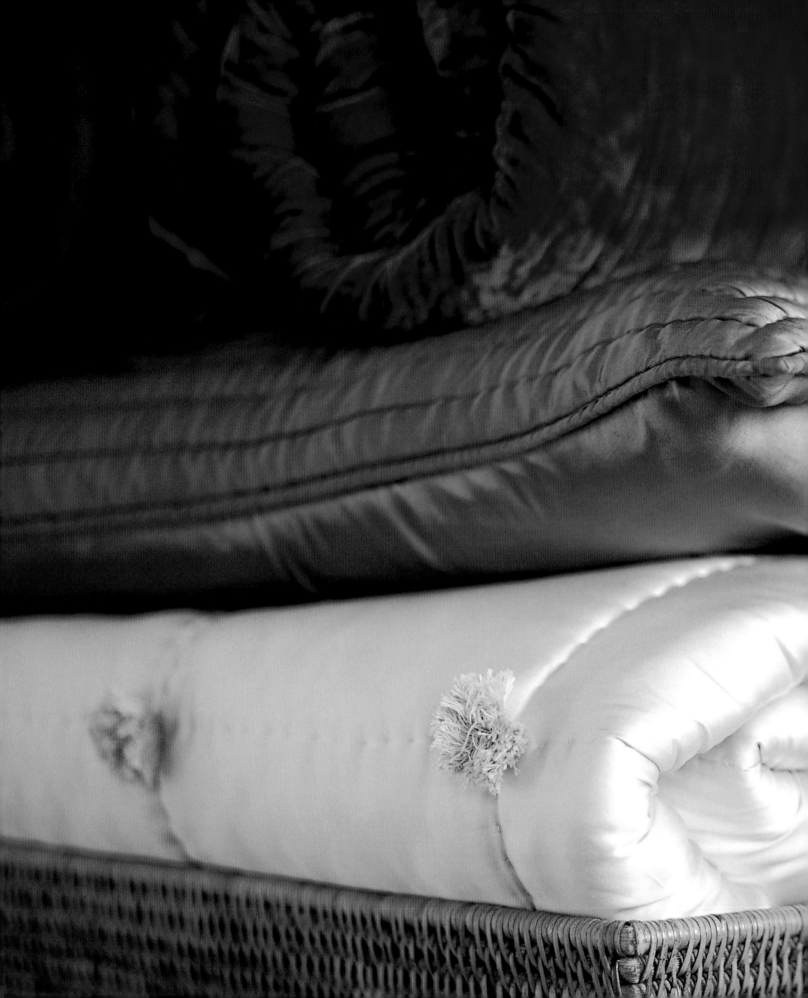

accessories

Accessories are expressions of your spirit. They are touchstones for memory, the items that make a room come alive. They can also be both decorative and practical, introducing accents of color into a room, enriching it with pattern and texture, or infusing a familiar setting with renewed energy and style.

Accessories come in every shape and size. Functional accessories like pillows and blankets serve a specific need. Bold accessories, such as large pieces of art, add drama. Personal accents, like mementos, photos, or quirky items brought currently interests you. Then feel free to change your focus. Change can be simple: switch lamp shades to alter the atmosphere; try adding a slipcover, some vibrant pillows, and a colorful, unexpected throw to renew a sofa. Or, simply rotate accessories within the room, or from one room to another to change both rooms at once.

Accessories also add seasonal variation and ambience. Drape a garland of vines or holiday lights over a mantel, or string crystal beads or pepper berries over a chandelier, and you instantly introduce a fresh spirit into the space.

A room should never be just a place to pass through. Use accessories to lend character to your space and offer a reason to stop and linger.

home from far-flung travels and flea markets, add character. Seasonal accessories give a room a change of pace. Whether set on the floor, hung on the walls or from the ceiling, or resting on a coffee table, accessories delight the eye and draw attention to different areas of the room.

Changing your accessories offers a simple and affordable way to evolve your style over time. As with a wardrobe, you can favor items for a season and then put them away. Weave fresh new hues through your space with colorful accents; introducing new rugs and drapes is much easier than painting walls. Use accessories to express your passion of the moment and to display whatever

The secret to accessorizing lies in finding interesting and surprising ways to bring things together, and to have fun doing it. Accessories don't need to be formal. They can be a casual expression of whimsy. Mix modern vases and picture frames with vintage game boards or primitive artworks. Display old hand mirrors or antique toys with fine crystal. Add natural objects (stones piled as a paperweight, a bowl of leaves on the credenza, a single fresh flower sewn to a sheaf of handmade card stock) to a sleek collection of silver candlesticks to create a palette of contrasting textures. Experiment fearlessly and with passion to imbue your living room with your own special style.

Adding Accessories for Warmth

Accessories populate a room and have a strong impact on how it feels. The right mix of pieces can lend interest to a large space and make it truly yours. Layers of color, soft textures, and intricate patterns are especially wise choices to temper the drama of a lofty architectural space.

When a room is larger than life, sometimes the instinct is to put a lot of furniture into it to bring it down to size. But the key to decorating a room like this is to create depth, and let the wonderful abundance of space be something to admire.

With well-planned zones to carve the room into livable areas, accessories add necessary warmth. Often it's the arrangement of accessories, as much as the items themselves, that creates a strong impression. Pairing items of differing colors, textures, and provenances draws attention to them. Creatively grouped accessories not only hold their place in a large room, they also arouse curiosity and make you want to draw near, whether to touch a translucent alabaster bowl or to sink into an inviting heap of pillows.

Accessories can change and evolve as you do, chronicling your interests like a three-dimensional scrapbook. Shelves offer opportunities to present interesting vignettes. Use them as you would a shadow box to combine the personal and the familiar with more exotic items: a postcard from a friend propped against a small painting, or leather-bound books comfortably arranged beside a modern vase.

Original artwork, *left*, is among the most personal of accessories. Unframed canvases leaning on a shelf can seem more approachable than when hung. **A daybed beckons**, *right*, in this reader's corner. A tousle of pillows in varied materials — wool kilim, leather, and silk — promises comfort. Overhead, paintings, artifacts, and antique books invite closer inspection.

The living room is the central gathering place of the home, and often the first space visitors see. Accessories placed at every level of the room create a sense of personality and comfort, and the items displayed provide a window into the heart of the collector. In this room, accessories inhabit even unexpected places. Dried botanicals and an original painting add impact to a high mantel; glazed wooden drums give appeal to a fireplace even when it's not in use; layered kilim rugs bring warmth and color to a polished cement floor. The rough texture of kilim pillows contrasts with the smooth faux-suede upholstery of the sofas.

Mirrored partial walls, *left*, next to the windows flanking the fireplace, create the illusion of double windows. The imposing Rumford fireplace is tall and shallow, better for drawing smoke up and out and reflecting heat into the room. **A row of low stools**, *above*, is a clever alternative to a console table behind the sofa and doubles as child-friendly seating.

Dressed for entertaining: candlelight enhances the luster of polished wood and silky pillows for a change of ambience.

By evening, the rustic character of this room is transformed. Accessories with nighttime appeal are brought in to add festive elegance and are shown at their best in candlelight. In lieu of a glowing fire, pillar candles of various heights stand on glazed drums in the fireplace. Glass vases that held feathery boughs earlier in the day become hurricane shades at night, encircling more pillars. Votives on the coffee table throw flashes of light across the brilliant sheen of silk pillows on the sofas.

Use candlelight as an accessory to create pockets of warmth and light wherever you'd like people to gather. Make sure there are plenty of metal cachepots, glass vases, and other objects with reflective surfaces around the room to keep light shimmering throughout the entire space.

Silk and velvet pillows, *left*, in fiery colors enhance a candlelit setting with their perfect sheen. **A group of glazed wooden drums**, *right*, is a surprising sculptural display in the fireplace. The fireplace surround is highlighted with subtly deepening shades of gray.

Color Palette

Blue walls, orange accents, and gray floors create a palette of warm and cool contrasts in this redwood-framed home. The sand-colored faux-suede upholstery and black mantel detailing complement the palette. Strong, saturated tones of terra-cotta, red, and orange (in the rugs, pillows, and throws) represent the heat of fire. Balanced with the neutral colors of the upholstery and floors, they infuse the room with spirited warmth. The redwood's hues also add to the room's warm, welcoming feeling.

Along with the rhythms of this room's artwork and collections, materials add a strong undercurrent of dimension and much of the room's color. The polished cement floor, redwood mouldings, and upholstery fabrics, including faux suede on the sofa, are all chosen to serve as a subtle neutral backdrop. This lets the vibrant patterns and rough, nubby woolens of kilim pillows and rugs take center stage.

Layering smaller rugs over one another establishes an informal feeling that one large area rug can't match. Small rugs also move easily to accommodate traffic in different areas. All the colors in the room can be found in the palette of the rugs – a unifying effect despite their complex tapestry of geometric patterns.

Materials

Kilims These richly patterned tapestries are woven of coarse, thick wools. Originally designed to be placed on sandy desert floors by nomadic peoples of countries such as Iran, Iraq, Pakistan, and Turkey, kilim rug patterns represent different tribes and regions. All are rich, vibrant, and geometric, and complement contemporary interiors.

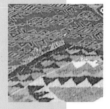

Faux suede Designed to mimic the touch of genuine suede, this durable, washable synthetic fabric is luxurious to the eye and hand. Made of microfibers, it contributes a soft, lush feeling to rooms.

Redwood While any wood that produces a red dye is considered a redwood, the most famous comes from coast redwoods, which grow up to 360 feet high. The wood's warm color creates a strong presence as it defines a room's geometry.

Large, clear glass vases, *left*, on the mantel are filled with dried eucalyptus. An original chalk and pastel painting suits the grand scale of the fireplace. The oversized coffee table is made from a carved wooden door. **Patterns of sunlight,** *above*, play across kilim and cotton pillows. Pillows are great quick-change accessories that can take a room from formal to comfortable in a snap.

Bringing the Outdoors In

An all-white room looks beautiful and clean with accessories in a natural palette. Look for flowers and other elements in many shades of white; in this palette, more is more. Bring in botanicals in shades of green for fresh accents of color, and add reflective glass and metal for shine.

All-white rooms are challenging and intriguing because everything you add to them is thrown into high contrast. Shape and texture are more prominent when colors are pale, so try choosing accessories with nature as your guide. Not only can you exhibit a profusion of forms gleaned from the world just outside your door, but these accessories also change easily according to the season.

Decorating in white alters the perception of space, so that small objects seem to come forward more than they would in a room with a more colorful palette. This is why an all-white room presents a special opportunity to feature simple, delicate forms that might get lost in a busier space.

An evolving display of clear, sculptural glass vessels, galvanized metal planters, and simple leaves and flowers keeps this room fresh, engaging, and in touch with the seasons. Architectural elements, brickwork, and the mantel are wrapped in an envelope of flat white paint, so that the furniture and the reflective and colored accessories take on more distinct silhouettes.

Textures and hues from nature, *left*, take on importance in this all-white room. A cotton matelassé throw, crisp twill slipcover, and green denim pillow invite you to settle in. **Boxwood topiaries in galvanized buckets**, *right*, and an English gathering basket bring a sense of the garden indoors. On the mantel, a botanical print, flowers from the garden, and potted ivy inside an antique lamp globe continue the horticultural theme.

The tones of white change as the quality of light shifts throughout the day and the seasons. The surface qualities of accessories also appear to alter in this changing light. The green ivy inside an old lamp globe actually becomes more visible in low light; the reflective glass globe itself takes prominence when the sun is high.

Shiny or matte, new or worn, accessories from the garden bring textural and visual depth to an all-white living space.

Because textures, like colors, have a perceived temperature of warm or cool, it's interesting to experiment with combinations of these elements to echo the seasons. A pure white matelassé throw looks crisp in the summer because of its hue, but warm in the winter because of its texture. A round dark wood table has an especially warm tone against cool white slipcovers, but in the bright noonday sun, its glazed finish gives it a slick polish that's in keeping with the room's cool temperature.

Open-plan architecture, *left*, in this barn-inspired living space is a natural setting for botanical accessories, which were chosen for their shapes, rather than for full-out color. **Rows of topiaries**, *right*, create an indoor version of a formal garden.

Design Details

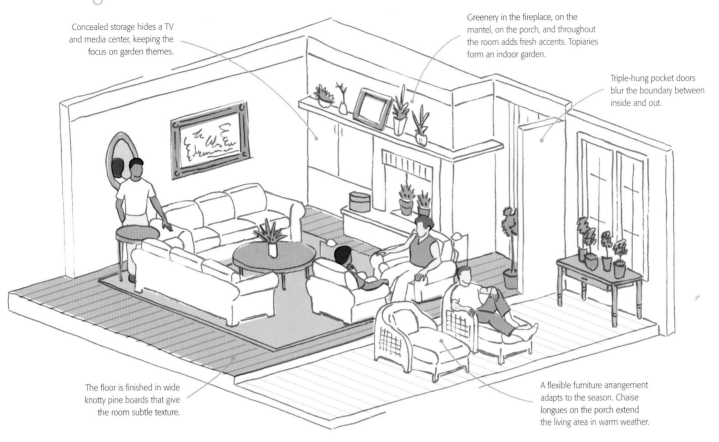

Concealed storage hides a TV and media center, keeping the focus on garden themes.

Greenery in the fireplace, on the mantel, on the porch, and throughout the room adds fresh accents. Topiaries form an indoor garden.

Triple-hung pocket doors blur the boundary between inside and out.

The floor is finished in wide knotty pine boards that give the room subtle texture.

A flexible furniture arrangement adapts to the season. Chaise longues on the porch extend the living area in warm weather.

Color Palette

Nature's colors – white, green, and brown – invite the outside world indoors. Like a leafy bouquet, green has many hues: sage green, with hints of silver; deep blue-green, the color of forest firs; and spring green, with its energetic yellow tones. Change the green accessories in an all-white room to suit the season. The soft brown tones of pine planks and a sisal rug are neutrals in the truest sense, blending well with most other hues.

Room Plan

Accessories and plants emphasize the summer garden theme. Greenery in stainless steel planters fills the fireplace; miniature topiaries populate a rustic wood farmhouse table. Casual, frayed-edge cotton pillows and a botanical print framed by weathered barn wood over the fireplace add green accents. During the warmer months, the pocket doors that separate the porch from the living room remain open. When the weather cools, the doors are closed and the club chairs are turned inward toward the fireplace.

Materials

White denim This durable upholstery fabric is casual yet sophisticated in white.

Sisal This natural fiber comes from the leaf of the agave plant. Woven into rugs, sisal makes a durable, casual, and stain-resistant flooring choice.

Matelassé With a woven raised pattern, this textile mimics the look of a quilt. Repeat washings soften it. A matelassé throw adds warm texture, even in white.

A Change of Climate

Echoing the changing seasons, this room has two personalities: one for warm weather and one for cool. You can reinvent a room without a lot of effort by simply focusing on accessories. Anchored by neutrals, a room can shift smoothly from open-aired and sunny to enclosed and autumnal.

Think of your living room as precisely that – a *living* room – an organic entity growing, evolving, and responding to the progress of the seasons. You can effect seasonal change on several levels. Certainly, replacing furniture or playing with different furniture groupings will transform a room. However, the simplest route to change is to swap out accessories with an eye toward rich accents of color.

Neutral-toned furniture, off-white walls, and natural floor coverings act as a blank canvas in this room, providing plenty of leeway for recasting the space according to the calendar. In spring and summer, splashes of yellow and green refresh the room with a cool, crisp style. Bold works of art and bright, geometric-patterned pillows create a relaxed space during the warm months. Bring in fresh flowers and spring-green plants of various textures to celebrate the bounty of the season. Shelf displays can be left more open to create a sense of airiness, allowing light-colored ceramics and objects to dominate. Keep window treatments sheer and breezy to allow as much light in as possible. As fall arrives, you can shed the citrus colors and green plants for a warmer, richer autumnal palette.

Citrus-inspired green and yellow accents, *left,* make this white interior feel as refreshing as a sip of lemonade. Shelf displays have plenty of breathing room, and the entire space is airy and open. **A lightweight waffle-weave blanket**, *right,* echoes the color of a boldly patterned linen pillow.

Decorate with seasonal ingredients. Replace summer's abundance of flowers and greenery with woodsy textures and winter berries.

Here, the living room has been transformed for winter – without changing any furniture. Spicy accents of red and gold recast the neutral backdrop to create a room that wraps you in warmth. The white slipcovers come off, and the space is layered with tactile delights: wool throws, lushly textured pillows, and a plush area rug atop the coir. Winter's textures brought in from the outdoors are naturally rougher than summer's: dried branches and berries bring deep, rich texture to the space.

Lighting is an important element, too. Whereas summer lighting tends to be clear and brilliant, a winter lighting scheme wants to be diffuse and more mellow. Lower the wattage with dimmers wherever possible; let accent lights and firelight add a soft glow.

Winter berries, *left,* bring delicate points of color to a fiery-hued palette. **Deep reds and earthy golds,** *right,* warm the room for winter. To make it even cozier, fill up shelves with dark, sculptural objects, dim the lights, and build a roaring fire.

Design Details

Color Palette

Citrus yellow accents and rejuvenating green accessories against a neutral white background celebrate spring. White denim slipcovers make it easy to swap out accessories to match the season while keeping the basics in place. A white ceramic platter of lemons next to a vase of spiky papyrus forms a still life that repeats the colors of the painting above the hearth and the flamelike fern in the fireplace. Green geometrically patterned pillows and a waffle-weave throw add colored texture.

Materials

White denim This durable cotton fabric is a great washable slipcover option for living or family rooms. White adds sophistication to this traditionally casual fabric, which will soften with repeated washings.

Waffle-weave cotton Recessed squares give this knit fabric a honeycomb texture that breathes easily.

Color Palette

Instill a feeling of fall with a color palette based on warm shades of earthy golds and deep reds against an adaptable winter white backdrop. The autumn-toned squares of a wool rug layered over a natural-colored coir rug pick up the deep chestnut of the modern, stained bamboo-veneer table. Winter berries and a harvest wreath contribute seasonal colors. A red blanket and tawny-toned cushions invite relaxation. A fire warms the room and lights the autumn palette.

Materials

Bamboo Made from a hollow-stemmed, woody grass, a stained bamboo veneer gives the coffee table a smooth, modern look in a warm chestnut color.

Wool rug A traditional fiber for carpet and rugs, wool is durable, insulating, and soil resistant. It also holds dye, such as this warm palette of autumn hues, well.

display

Display is about being proud of the things you own, and showing them off with passion. Whether it's a collection of family portraits, vintage vases, model cars, or shards of beach glass, display lends everyday objects a sense of importance, and gives especially prized items the attention they deserve.

Arranging a personal collection can seem daunting, but it's not complicated. Think about how you want to interact with favored possessions. They can be conveniently at hand and easily rearranged, or placed out of harm's way.

an eclectic range of photos can be identically matted and framed to create a cohesive display on a wall or mantel. A series of diverse but similarly shaped pieces can become a provocative group if they're lined up uniformly along a ledge.

Choosing where you wish to showcase a collection is also important. Hanging a series of photos or artworks close to the back of a sofa, low along the wall, strengthens their visual relationship. Displays that are eye level, such as along a tall sideboard or a mid-level shelf, are perceived as more active than those above or below eye level.

The possessions in a room tell a unique story. Displaying the objects you love creates a personal environment, filled with hopes and memories.

On a table or low ledge, up high or under glass, on shelves or in frames – choose systems that help you enjoy the objects you love most.

Repetition creates interest, and displaying objects in multiples can be quite dramatic. But anything you enjoy or appreciate can become a collection if you unify the items with a consistent display idea. Experiment with color and material. Try mixing two- and three-dimensional pieces that share a color palette or are made of similar materials to create a vivid, layered pastiche.

Objects that are related by shape alone can also make interesting displays. Though they may come from disparate places and points of view,

Be focused about what you feature in your living room, and try to avoid having too many objects competing with one another. Paring down your choices to just a few things that are important to you can result in a more attractive display.

As seasons change, so can the stories you tell in your rooms. In the autumn, bring in colorful leaves, berries, and branches to create a casual coffee table arrangement. If you've just returned from a trip, change the focus to show recently acquired souvenirs or artworks. Reward kids' artistic efforts by giving their projects pride of place. In so doing, you make your room a reflection of who you are and what's important to you.

Moving Pictures

Think of your living room as your personal gallery, where you can create a changing display that captures your life, passions, and ideals. Pictures don't have to be singular or static; fill an entire wall with favorites – family and friends, memories, and places you dream of.

Creating displays filled with personal meaning is easier than you may think. To begin, focus on how you want your room to function. Is it a place for quiet relaxing, or for bringing the family together? Is it an active entertainment zone, or a realm for private conversation? The displays you create should suit the environment of the room.

Next, concentrate on things that intrigue you, and consider how you can share your interests in a way that's in keeping with the room's scale and style. A photo wall is a great way to do this. Here, a love of film inspires a room where both personal memories and cinematic dreams come to life. On one wall, a large personal gallery mimics the style of movie production stills to showcase a collection of scenes from family life. Reproduced in various sizes but similarly framed, this wall of memories has a consistent – but energetic – feel. The images can easily be replaced or moved as experiences accumulate and favorite memories change. In keeping with the theme, a row of salvaged theater seats steeps the room in Hollywood history, and an old movie reel becomes a clever lazy Susan for popcorn and other snacks.

A passion for the movies, *left*, creates a room full of whimsy. Black-and-white family photos tell a dramatic story when arranged en masse on a single wall. **A collection of old cameras**, *right*, shares the mantel with vintage movie posters, forming a layered display of related elements.

A wide wall-to-wall sofa bench stacked with pillows faces a projection video screen, creating an elegantly laid-back viewing platform. A large leather ottoman can double as both a snack table and seating; burgundy velvet floor-to-ceiling drapes swathe the windows, evoking the look and feel of a movie theater. The unusual seating options transform the room into a great space for entertaining. When it's not being used for movie viewing, the sofa bench's placement by the windows offers plenty of natural light for reading.

A large projection screen, *above*, slides down over the room's pocket doors to conserve space. **A row of cameras**, *right*, faces a wall of photos, while the photos gaze back at the cameras, adding a dose of humor. A room needn't be completely serious to be taken seriously.

Design Details

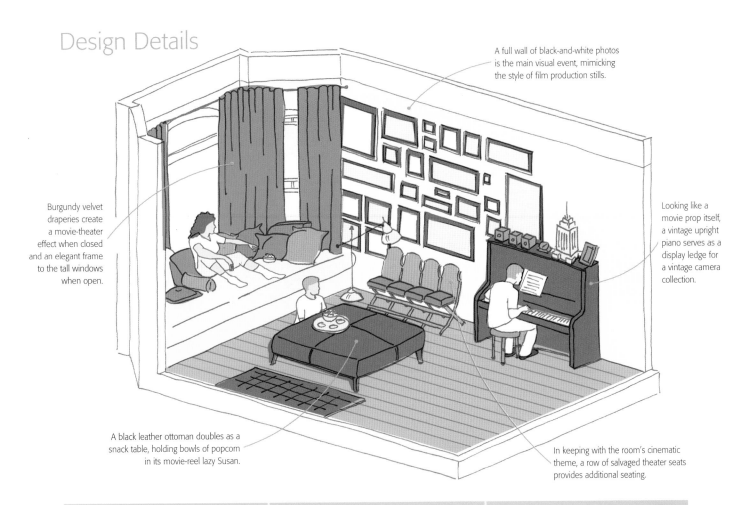

A full wall of black-and-white photos is the main visual event, mimicking the style of film production stills.

Burgundy velvet draperies create a movie-theater effect when closed and an elegant frame to the tall windows when open.

Looking like a movie prop itself, a vintage upright piano serves as a display ledge for a vintage camera collection.

A black leather ottoman doubles as a snack table, holding bowls of popcorn in its movie-reel lazy Susan.

In keeping with the room's cinematic theme, a row of salvaged theater seats provides additional seating.

Color Palette

Pale yellow, burgundy, and slick black set the scene in a room designed for viewing films. Burgundy velvet drapes play off the movie-theater decor and envelop the space in drama. Pale yellow walls temper the fabric's darkness and offer a neutral backdrop for movie-themed displays. A leather ottoman echoes the black in the artwork. Although the room's furnishings are contemporary, its mix of deep, sober colors suits its Victorian architecture.

Room Plan

A long platform bench set into a bay window is the room's main seating area and preferred movie-viewing perch (a projection screen pulls down over the room's pocket doors, opposite the bench). Topped with faux-suede–wrapped futons and a multitude of pillows in soft, lustrous patterns and solids, the generous sofa is as comfortable as a well-feathered nest. Tucking the custom-built sofa into the window nook and using a pull-down screen leaves most of the room's walls open for displays, which can be seen and appreciated from the viewing bench.

Materials

Velvet A low, cut-pile weave creates a luxurious texture. The weave's density makes velvet an ideal drapery fabric for screening out light.

Leather Tanned animal hides withstand wear without tearing. Especially when dyed deep colors, leather is a good upholstery fabric.

Faux suede This man-made fabric, resembling leather with a napped surface, offers a soft, washable upholstery option for sofas and chairs.

A Clean Slate for Display

A contemporary space may be architecturally powerful, but it's the objects and collections within that give it emotional energy. Think of a lofty white space as a blank canvas waiting for bold strokes. Place displays at every level, on every surface, to create a rich visual vocabulary.

A living room is a natural home for a display wall. In contemporary settings, a display can almost take the place of a hearth, influencing the placement of furniture and providing a center of focus for the room. Even a simple composition can say a lot in a modern interior, especially if it has an element of surprise to it.

Offhand, casual arrangements are a quick way to dress up a room, and their impermanence makes them interesting. For displays of this type, any blank wall makes the perfect canvas – a place where you can simply lean pictures, framed or not. There is great creative freedom in being able to experiment without having to measure or make holes in the wall. Try layering different-sized pieces of art, so that each image is a foil to the next.

In this loftlike space, the theme of transportation links a collection of objects and photos, softening the room's angles with colorful focal points. Arranged on tabletops, hung on walls, perched on shelves, placed on the floor, and clipped to wire, the multilevel display is dynamic and easy to change.

A trio of glass vases, *left*, catches sunlight and adds color and sculptural form to the room's display. **The lively touch of red**, *right*, unifies this casual collection of artwork and objects. The stacked arrangement of the prints is pleasingly asymmetrical. Hanging one, leaning another, and standing the third on the shelf adds dimension and dynamism.

A successful display has presence, whether a single object, a simple grouping, or a full collection. It stops the eye and captures the imagination.

When we view a display, we look instinctively for ways to organize the objects into a visual hierarchy. The practice of layering artworks is effective in defining this hierarchy, and lets you determine each piece's prominence. Some artworks can hang from the wall; other pieces may be mounted to the fronts of shelves to bring them closer to the viewer. This three-dimensional layering not only makes the display more visually pleasing, it also opens up new possibilities for display. Picture arrangements needn't be limited to the tops of shelves; the undersides of shelves can be used as well to suspend artworks and keepsakes.

The theme of transportation, *left,* is a driving force behind the displays in this light-filled space. Framing photographs all in black and white also unifies this varied, multileveled wall display. **A simple arrangement of yarrow**, *left and above,* makes a distinctly modern flower display.

To appear cohesive, a display needs only a single common element, whether shape, size, color, material, or motif. Here, cars, trains, and roadways unite a collection. Keying off the theme, the color palette plays a supporting role and extends the motif with subliminal wit: reds, yellows, and greens – the colors of traffic lights – dominate.

To maintain the focus of a collection, it's best not to combine too many elements in one display. Leaving some empty space, especially within dense displays, allows the pieces to breathe. Unpopulated areas can speak as loudly as objects, directing the viewer's attention to the pieces at hand.

Simple shelves, *left,* are thoughtfully installed to shape a dynamic display. The shelves are graduated in width to provide maximum flexibility in layering artworks. **Binder clips and wire**, *above,* are a creative alternative to mats and frames. Their style is more casual, and you can match the color of the clips to the artwork. They also make it easy to change your display as often as you'd like.

Design Details

Color Palette

A contemporary, graphic palette of bright white, pure red, and metallic gray complements this loft space beautifully. Swept with a simple coat of white, the living room walls become a clean canvas for collections of color photography and multihued glass vessels. As the light changes throughout the day, white takes on subtle tints: from rose to blue or lavender gray. The changing hues emphasize the red-accented collections and accessories to dramatic effect, and highlight the brilliant colors in the photos.

Materials

Galvanized metal Metal is galvanized by adding one thin layer of metal over another metal to prevent corrosion. Showing the resulting mottled finish in a room by exposing metal ductwork lends a raw, industrial feel to the space.

Painted brick An exposed brick wall contributes to a loft's industrial look. Painting the rougher brick the same bright white as the smooth, plasterboard walls helps emphasize the room's spaciousness and offers a contrasting texture.

Glass Generally made of minerals called silicates, glass describes a type of material with a liquidlike molecular structure that, when melted and cooled, becomes rigid without crystallizing. Glassblowers heat glass until it's soft, blow air through a tube into the glass to shape it into vessels like this room's vases, and then cool it rapidly.

How to Style Shelves

STYLE IDEAS

Walls can be much more than a backdrop. If you have shelves or ledges, think of them as a stage waiting for props. To style them, clear some space and give your collection plenty of room. Edit your choices, selecting just a few pieces so that each is shown to its best advantage. Arrange favorite objects in levels: low, medium, and high. Groups of three are also attractive, as are slightly off-center arrangements.

Colorful displays, *opposite page*, are especially striking when all the items are made of the same material, such as glass or stone. This unifies a collection, and lets you play with sizes and shapes to produce a sculptural effect. Here, glass vases from the 1950s and '60s are mixed with Venetian glass and a modern stool. Though each vase is unique, the limited color palette and repetition of organic shapes tie them together.

A monochromatic collection, *this page,* is unified by hue rather than material. Opting for all white brings together many different styles and silhouettes. It also highlights the beautiful surface texture of each piece. Vary the tonal range from ivory to pure white, blue-white to bone. Place larger items at the bottom to create a balanced composition that draws the eye upward. Here, a collection of white porcelain, an old glove mold, white books, clear glass, and black-and-white photos produce a sleek effect.

How to Arrange Displays

Eclectic objects become a cohesive display when you find ways to unify them. Once you've chosen the spot for your display – on a wall, along a mantel, on a tabletop, or stepped at various levels – you can group objects with a similar or complementary color, material, shape, or theme. Objects may lend themselves to a formal display that relies on symmetry, or they might call out for an offhand presentation. Arranging objects in groups of three or five makes a visually pleasing display; asymmetrical arrangements are visually intriguing. A mix of two- and three-dimensional objects can harmonize if they echo one another's period or style.

A collection of black-and-white portraits, *left,* is easily unified with a consistent style of mat and frame. **A whimsical display system**, *top,* made from a dried tree branch and paper clips, allows you to change photos and mementos whenever the spirit moves you. **A vintage hotel sign,** *above,* is layered between pictures. Arranged in descending height along a rough mantel, each object seems to create a mat for the next. Even the impromptu sculpture made from a simple pile of stones shares the same color palette, another effective display practice.

An asymmetric display, *left,* lends a collection of artwork a casual feel. The size and weight of the old frames gives the grouping a sense of unity. **Stepped displays**, *below,* place three-dimensional items in the foreground of hanging art, which helps to frame the grouping. Echoing the shape of the girl in the painting, or repeating the subjects on the canvas, *bottom,* creates compelling resonances that make these displays coherent.

Room Resources

At Pottery Barn, we believe that casual style is something you can weave through every space in your home, from front rooms to private havens. For this book, we scoured hundreds of locations to find perfect settings to create rooms just for you. We experimented with colors, furnishings, rugs, drapes, and accessories to find the best combinations for each space. The results? This collection of style ideas, which we hope will inspire and delight you.

Each location chosen for this book was unique and interesting. Here is a little bit more about each of the homes we visited, the style ideas we created, and the individual elements that make each design tick.

A note about color: wherever it was possible in this list of resources, we've offered the actual paint manufacturer and paint color that was used in the room shown. We also list the closest Benjamin Moore paint color match (in parentheses). Because photography and color printing processes can dramatically change the way colors appear, it is very important to test swatches of any paint color you are considering in your own home where you can see how the light affects them at different times of the day.

Room for Living

This sunny, open-plan space is part of a ranch retreat for a large family. Walls have been removed to open the kitchen to the living room and paned glass doors were added along the length of the expanded great room to open it to the outdoors.

Space Living room/kitchen is 36' long x 23' wide. Floorboards are 11"-wide knotty pine planks. Beams and ceiling supports are exposed throughout the house. Above the paned glass doors, heavy-gauge wire takes the place of curtain rods and makes floor-length linen drapes easy to open and close.

Color Walls and ceilings (Benjamin Moore OC-64, Pure White flat). Focal wall (Benjamin Moore Bull's Eye Red 2002-20 flat).

Furnishings Fringed jute rug, tuffet beanbag, lambswool rug, gallery picture frames, all from Pottery Barn. Custom-made bench sofas; bench cushions are twin-size, linen-covered futons. Custom dining table and chalkboard coffee table designed by Celia Tejada. Vintage café chairs and leather armchair.

Lighting Task lights by Artemide. Disc halogen wire-track lights at kitchen island.

pages 14–21

Rooms Within a Room

Once a tiny saltbox, this cottage was expanded and remodeled in 1992. An added wing includes a master bedroom suite, downstairs guest bedroom and bath, powder room, and front hall.

Space The living room features two-story ceilings and a loft that's a home office/sleeping suite. The main seating area is 21' x 23'. The house was designed by Richard Martino and architect Will Schulz (Southampton, NY).

Color Benjamin Moore Atrium White Interior Ready Mixed 79 flat, with semi-gloss on ledges.

Furnishings Throw, leather pillows, Cortland floor lamp, and ribbon lamp shades, all from Pottery Barn. Cotton sailcloth sofas by Jean Michel Frank. Pavilion coffee table by Mies van der Rohe. Plywood chair by Charles and Ray Eames. Heywood-Wakefield buffet with winemaking bottle and Russell Wright ceramic dish. Turned wood vessels and 1700s Irish pine cupboard. Driftwood primitive chair.

Display Cowboys photograph (above window seat) and snapshot (above chest) by Arthur Elgort (Marianne, New York, NY). *Mirror* gelatin silver print by Laura Larson (Lennon, Weinberg Gallery, New York, NY).

pages 26–33

A Small Space

Originally little more than a cabin, this hillside cottage lacked plumbing and had fallen into disrepair. Newly remodeled, the building now includes a wraparound porch and a formal front garden.

Space The original pre-fabricated structure is circa 1940. The remodeled cottage is 850 square feet with interior details inspired by local barn architecture: a cathedral ceiling, sheet plywood walls with batting, and wide-plank pine floors. The living room is 19' x 11'.

Color Walls, trim, and ceiling: Benjamin Moore Swiss Coffee OC-45 satin.

Furnishings Charleston loveseat in twill, Megan chairs in denim, Farmhouse occasional tables, Prairie bench, vintage map print, gallery frame and clip frames, fringed denim pillow, all from Pottery Barn. Vintage wicker chair, Cremo Biscuit chest as side table, vintage steamer trunk, tortoise-finish bamboo and wicker occasional table, farmhouse table, pine-framed mirror, vintage 45-rpm record player, records, and metal lunch box.

Lighting Wire cage lamp with Pottery Barn ribbon lamp shade, vintage floor lamp, souvenir-bottle lamp from Chicago World's Fair.

pages 34–39

Living with Color

Just a short walk from the Atlantic Ocean, this stately, shingled two-story house has an adjacent guest cottage and pool. The living room has a view of a large garden with formal clipped hedges.

Space The comfortable den is 15' x 14' and has an 8' ceiling that is finished in white-painted beadboard paneling. A galley kitchen adjoins the room.

Color Walls (Benjamin Moore Yellow Highlighter 2021-40). Trim (Benjamin Moore Snow White OC-66 gloss).

Furnishings Nantucket buffet, Manhattan leather sofa and armchairs, accordion lamp shades, and cocktail shaker, all from Pottery Barn. Vintage clock collection and metal watchmaker's cabinet. Diamond-quilted velvet seat cushion courtesy of The Village Latch Inn. Art Deco–style lacquer coffee table courtesy of Homenature, Amagansett, NY. Clock hands, Zora bar, and seltzer-bottle lamp courtesy of Lauren Copen Antiques, Bridgehampton, NY.

Display Horse painting by David Rudd, courtesy of Mark Humphrey Gallery, Southampton, NY. Oil portrait courtesy of Privet Cove, Southampton, NY.

pages 46–51

A Natural Home for Texture

Tucked in a garden courtyard, this 2,700-square-foot Mediterranean-style villa is flanked by a guest house and office space. The villa's architecture was inspired by an old Florida estate.

Space The 26'-long living room has three pairs of 8' French doors. The fireplace surround is antique limestone, salvaged from a French chateau and cut down to fit the current space. Floors and wood trim are mahogany throughout. (Contact the Rainforest Alliance to learn about responsibly harvested rare woods.)

Color Walls (Benjamin Moore Simply White 2143-70 flat).

Furnishings Valencia daybed, PB Basic twill chair, chunky cotton throw, pandan pillows, tufted twill pillows, Sierra suede pillow shams, Stella rose duvet, solid voile sheer drapes, tie-top linen drapes, and rustic metal rods and rings, all from Pottery Barn. 1940s-era baby buggy wheels (on mantel). Coir rug layered with fleece. Velvet tuffet, vintage metal teapot. On sofa: Indian cotton print throw, shibori pillow, and beaded blue silk pillow.

Lighting Recessed lights in ceiling.

Display *Shipyard series #4,* abstract oil and charcoal on canvas by Susan Spies.

pages 62–67

Vacation-Style Comfort

Built for a large extended family, this mountaintop vacation retreat enjoys spectacular views. Its open-plan main building was inspired, in part, by traditional Polynesian longhouse architecture.

Space The living room is 40' x 28', with a 12' ceiling. Double doors at each end of the space are 8'. Doors flanking the fireplace are Dutch-style, with a single pane over a solid panel.

Color Integral color plaster walls. Cedar beams and exposed support structure. Sealed and waxed integral-color cement floors. Redwood fireplace mantel.

Furnishings PB Basic twill sofas and ottomans, camp lanterns, tripod lamp, and fringed denim pillow covers, all from Pottery Barn. Pottery Barn Schoolhouse dining chairs and vintage mismatched chairs at 12' refectory table. Antique apothecary bottles. Teak Indonesian bed platform. Stoneware pickling crocks on mantel. Mudroom: Pottery Barn Amelia entryway bench, vintage cola storage crates, 1950s "Alaska" ice cream maker, picnic baskets, and minnow buckets.

Lighting 24" iron ring chandeliers. Wire-track halogen (in dining area). Ceiling-mounted spotlights.

Display Vintage globe collection.

pages 76–83

A Warm Reception

On a tree-lined street in a gracious suburban setting, this custom-built two-story home includes an in-law suite, a gourmet kitchen, and a screened porch. The living room opens onto a spacious entryway and dining room.

Space The fireplace is 48" tall, with a generous, faux-stone surround. The living room is 15' x 16'.

Color Walls (Benjamin Moore Kingsport Gray HC-86 flat). Trim (Benjamin Moore Cloud White OC-130 semigloss).

Furnishings Metropolitan console table, Mesa everydaysuede™ pillow, Sullivan leather ottoman, pillar candles and tapers, and woven wood baskets, all from Pottery Barn. George Smith sofa. Faux-bamboo armoire. Velvet and silk throw; paisley throw and pillow. Button-tufted leather club chair. Turned wood bowl and spool candlesticks.

Lighting Recessed ceiling lighting. Pottery Barn double-stem adjustable lamp and table lamp.

Display Pottery Barn *Red Mixed Media* painting by Edward Peterson.

pages 94–99

Summer Sun, Winter Warmth

This shingled, classic California Craftsman cottage was built circa 1910. Recently remodeled and updated, the house is located on a steep slope planted with terraced rock gardens in front and back.

Space French doors open onto a porch at one end, extending the living room in warm weather. The front of the room is a wall of windows overlooking treetops that change with the seasons. Adjacent to the entryway, the living room opens onto a small library with a window seat.

Color Walls (Benjamin Moore Rich Cream 2153-60 flat). Trim (Benjamin Moore Mountain Peak White 2148-70 semigloss).

Furnishings PB Basic twill sofa and chair, solid voile sheer drapes, shirred organdy pillow cover (summer); chenille drapes layered with dupioni silk drapes, French-knot silk pillows, shimmer beaded pillow, pepperberry garland, and pillar candles (winter), all from Pottery Barn. Vintage garden patio table, steamer trunk, shoemaker's form, and juggling pins. Summer: birdcage with floral display. Winter: dried pomegranates, pheasant feathers, pepperberries, and ostrich egg in collector's case.

pages 108–15

A Place for Everything

This 2,600-square-foot, Provençal-style home sits on a two-acre lot dotted with madrone and oak trees. Vineyards surround the property. The architecture was inspired by buildings typical to the Rhone Valley in France.

Space Constructed with rammed earth, a centuries-old building method, this house has thick walls and deep-silled windows. Heating is passive solar. The pool provides natural cooling as breezes blow across the water and into the house. The tile entryway frieze is salvaged from a department store. The floor is terra tile: 1.5"-thick cast earth, sealed and waxed.

Color Bookcase (Benjamin Moore Smoke 2122-40 flat). Bookcase wall (Benjamin Moore White Wisp OC-54 flat).

Furnishings Isabelle sofa, Stafford bench, Tristan occasional table, and Airstream trailer model, all from Pottery Barn. Iron coat hooks are from Mexico. Handwoven basket, primitive wooden mortar, crackle-glaze pottery, cast bowl, and cowrie shell basket. Vintage leather Pullman case and black iron cashbox.

Lighting Recessed ceiling lights.

Display Two-panel oil on canvas painting (above fireplace) by Gail Chase-Bien.

pages 124–29

Storage for Everyone

In a new, spacious home custom-designed for a growing family, this den and adjoining play space open onto a large backyard. A screened porch is adjacent on the left side of the house, and an in-law suite is on the right.

Space French doors, high ceilings, and a wall of built-in media storage keep this room feeling spacious and uncluttered. The middle of the wall cabinet hides a television and stereo system; drawers for storing videos and CDs are below. Architecture: Moller Willrich Architecture, San Francisco, CA.

Color Walls (Benjamin Moore Beacon Hill Damask HC-2). Trim (Benjamin Moore Cloud White OC-130).

Furnishings Westport sectional sofa, fringed denim pillow covers, colorbound seagrass rug, white chenille pillow sham, and Airstream trailer model, all from Pottery Barn. Chalkboard totes, rolling wicker storage cart, Dollhouse bookshelf, and Carolina chair, all from Pottery Barn Kids. Vintage schoolroom desk and chair, and wooden alphabet blocks.

Lighting Recessed ceiling lights.

pages 130–35

Accessories for Warmth

This John Marsh Davis house began with a garden. The architect lived on-site in a cottage while he spent three years researching and creating the landscape design. The house was later designed and built around the finished garden.

Space The 2,800-square-foot main house shares the property with a guest cottage, a children's playhouse, and an artist's studio. Walls are old-growth redwood, harvested only from naturally fallen trees. Ceiling is fir. Floors are sealed concrete. Doors fashioned by Davenport Mill, Santa Cruz, CA.

Color Walls (Benjamin Moore Buckland Blue HC-151).

Furnishings Travis sofa, Brava trunk, and leather pillows, all from Pottery Barn. On window seat ledge: French wooden bowl covered in goatskin, Iron Asian temple candlestick, and alabaster candlestick. Custom-designed coffee table from an Indonesian teak door. Javanese drums (in fireplace).

Lighting The ceiling skylight is specially designed to modulate light in summer and reflect more light in winter. Industrial pendant lights. Haley floor lamp with soft square shade from Pottery Barn.

Display All paintings by Karen Barbour.

pages 142–49

Bringing the Outdoors In

This hillside country house has views of vineyards and architecture inspired by a swallow barn. To help blur the line between inside and out, the Douglas fir floors have no thresholds – all windows and doors are pocket installations.

Space The 17' room is part of an open-plan lower floor that includes an entry hall, kitchen and dining area, and guest room and bath. A sunporch runs the full length of the house. Three hidden cabinets, at the left of the fireplace, hold television and stereo equipment.

Color Walls and ceilings: Fuller O'Brien White Wing flat (Benjamin Moore White Heron OC-57).

Furnishings PB Basic white denim sofa and chairs, fringed denim shams, and Elena matelassé coverlet, all from Pottery Barn. Antique pine farmhouse table. Pine refectory table. Boxwood in galvanized metal pails in hearth. Woven gathering basket. Mantel: antique gas light globe, ivy, weathered wood frame, pastel botanical drawing, handblown "genie" bottle, and antique wasp catcher.

Lighting Polished metal apothecary floor lamps. Wood-paneled ceiling has recessed lighting, including flip-down picture lights.

pages 150–55

A Change of Climate

Used as a second-home country getaway, this diminutive bungalow was completely remodeled to open up the interior space. The property includes a gazebo, a large lap pool, and a manicured garden. White roses line the yard.

Space The single-story house has 1,200 square feet of space. During remodeling, the interior was gutted and the ceilings were raised. The living room features a bank of French doors opening onto a generous deck shaded by a full-grown lemon tree. Vineyards and Western hills are visible in the distance. Consulting architect, Brooks Walker, Jr.

Color Custom-mixed color by Benjamin Moore (Benjamin Moore White Chocolate OC-127 flat).

Furnishings Vintage patchwork rug from Pottery Barn. Contemporary slipcovered sofa and chairs. Custom bamboo-finish coffee table. Sisal rug. Contemporary waffle-weave throw, pashmina throw, chenille throw, linen pillows, and velvet-and-silk pillows.

Lighting Track/halogen spotlights, Pottery Barn glass base lamp.

pages 156–61

Moving Pictures

Designed as a welcoming haven for family and friends, this display-rich den doubles as a movie-viewing room. On the first floor of a three-story Victorian townhouse, the den has formal front windows that look out on city views.

Space The high ceilings, fireplace, and tall "eyebrow" windows are common features of Victorian architecture. At the far end of the room, pocket doors open to a combination art studio and study. A large kitchen in the back of the house opens onto a sheltered garden courtyard.

Color Walls (Benjamin Moore Soft Beige 2156-60). Trim (Benjamin Moore White Opulence OC-69).

Furnishings Leather pillows, smocked velvet pillow covers, and velvet drapes, all from Pottery Barn. Vintage upright piano, movie theater bench seats, metal movie reel, and framed movie posters. Custom button-tufted seat cushions. Contemporary patterned velvet pillows and black leather square ottoman. Custom-made window seat bench covered in everydaysuede™.

Lighting Custom-designed swing-arm floor lamp.

Display Portrait-wall artwork and camera collection courtesy of the homeowner.

pages 166–71

A Clean Slate for Display

A city warehouse loft is home to this art lover's living room. The loft enjoys views of skyscrapers and the Statue of Liberty. A spiral metal staircase in the library leads to a rooftop photography studio and garden.

Space Exposed ductwork hints at the finished loft's industrial roots. A walk-in closet is in the center of the space.

Color Benjamin Moore Atrium White Interior Ready Mixed 79 flat. Semigloss ledges.

Furnishings Mies van der Rohe Barcelona chair and Pavilion coffee table.

Display Artwork reflects a transportation theme. Ledge, page 173: photorealistic painting by Robert Schmid courtesy of Sears-Peyton Gallery; car photo by David Martinez; stop sign tray by Borris Bally. Wall ledges and floor, page 174 (top to bottom, left to right): three car photos by Sheri Giblin; two photos from *New York City Subway Depots* series by Chris Faust; four Cibachrome photos by Scott M. Goldman; *NYC Kiss* photo by Cat Gwynn/www.guild.com/www.corbis.com; found postcard; bikes photo by Joseph De Leo; two photos from *Havana, Cuba,* series by David Martinez. Copyrights held by artists listed.

pages 172–77

Glossary

Bamboo A renewable and sustainable material, this hollow-stemmed woody grass is used in the manufacture of crushed bamboo rugs, matchstick blinds, furniture (as a veneer), and flooring.

Beadboard The most common type of wainscoting, beadboard gets its name from the regularly spaced bumps that are milled along the length of each piece. This form of wainscoting became widely available with the advent of industrial milling in the 1850s and was a popular feature of Victorian homes. Used on walls or furniture, it adds nostalgic charm.

Bento boxes These Japanese lacquered boxes are traditionally used for serving lunches, but can also store small items in the home or serve as trays.

Board-and-batten An early form of residential siding used to weatherproof log homes, this vertical plank siding became a characteristic detail of late eighteenth- and nineteenth-century Gothic Revival homes. It can be used to cover an entire house or as a decorative accent.

Canvas This durable fabric is commonly used for manufacturing sporting goods, awnings, and outdoor furnishings. When used for drapes, slipcovers, or pillows, it brings a relaxed feel to a room. Canvas can be made from linen, hemp, or cotton and is available bleached, unbleached, or in a variety of dyed hues.

Cement A term often used interchangeably with concrete, cement is actually a fine gray powder that is mixed with water, sand, and gravel to make concrete. It is also used to make stucco, plaster, mortar, and grout.

Chaise longue Literally "long chair," this chair with a sort of built-in ottoman comfortably supports outstretched legs.

Chenille Aptly named after the French word for "caterpillar," chenille weaves silk or cotton into tufted cords for greater depth and richness. This luxuriously nubby fabric is commonly used to make blankets. A soft chenille throw adds a cozy touch to a sofa, while chenille drapes give a plush feeling of warmth.

Coir This natural fiber is derived from the husks of coconuts, grown in Sri Lanka and other tropical locations. Once removed from the husks, the fiber is spun and machine-woven into matting, and often backed with latex for increased durability. A popular floor covering, coir is tough, resilient, and more textural than other natural-fiber rugs. It is an excellent rug choice in high-traffic areas. The color of coir varies based on its harvest time.

Concrete Cement, sand, water, and gravel form this strong, easy-to-maintain flooring material. Recent innovations in dyeing and tinting allow concrete to be made in any color and even etched with designs. No longer relegated just to roads, driveways, and curbs, concrete is being used to create countertops, fireplace surrounds, furniture, and interior flooring. Decorative finishes include acid etching, stamping, polishing, and staining.

Cotton twill Twill fabrics are characterized by a raised diagonal design and are noted for their firm, close weave. Denim is an example of cotton twill.

Denim Originally believed to be from France, this durable cotton fabric became popular in the United States during the California Gold Rush, in the form of work pants (jeans). It is also a great washable slipcover option for casual living rooms or family rooms, especially where kids and pets play. Repeated washings will soften the fabric and the traditional indigo color, adding to its appeal. White denim has a more sophisticated look.

Dupioni silk Woven from two threads of the same or different colors, dupioni silk shimmers and seems to change color in the light. The fabric is woven from an irregular, rough silk thread that is the result of two silkworms spinning the same cocoon. It has textural bumps, or "slubs," similar to those of raw silk.

Eames, Charles and Ray The American architect Charles Eames (1907–78) and his wife, artist Ray Eames (1912–88), are considered to be among the most influential designers of the twentieth century. Working collaboratively, the couple designed furniture, buildings, exhibitions, toys, and interiors. One tenet of their philosophy was that good design should be available to all, and they are probably best known for pioneering the use of molded plywood to mass-produce chairs, screens, and tables. Many of their designs have been reissued, and vintage pieces are considered highly collectible.

Faux fur This plush synthetic material feels as soft and warm as the real thing. No longer used just for coats and jackets, faux fur makes great plush throws and pillow covers.

Faux suede Designed to mimic the look and touch of genuine napped leather, this durable synthetic is luxurious to the eye and hand. Made of microfibers, it offers a soft, washable upholstery option for sofas and chairs, and contributes a soft, lush feeling to living rooms.

Fieldstone Rough-hewn stone, found in fields where the bedrock is close to the surface, fieldstone links a home to its natural surroundings. Stone in its natural form has a rustic hand-hewn quality, whereas quarry-cut stone is smoother and more regularly shaped.

Flat weave Created on a loom, a flat-weave rug is smoothly finished with no knots or pile, like a tapestry. A wool flat-weave rug such as a kilim is also often reversible and makes a durable floor covering for high-traffic areas.

Galvanized metal Metal is galvanized by coating it with a thin layer of another metal (usually zinc) to create a protective finish. It is often used to make ductwork or items such as tubs or light fixtures intended for outdoor use. The distinctive mottled finish of galvanized metal has a raw, industrial feel and can add character to a room when used indoors.

Glass Generally made of minerals called silicates, glass describes a type of material with a liquid-like molecular structure that, when melted and cooled, becomes rigid without crystallizing. While clear and colored glass allow light to shine through, other effects are also possible. Sand-blasted glass has a cooler, frosted look, while a semi-opaque glass diffuses light without fully blocking it.

Grosgrain This strong, close-woven fabric with prominent ribs is usually made of silk or rayon and often has cotton filler.

Jute A strong, woody plant fiber grown extensively in Asia, jute is noted for its innate strength and longevity. When woven, it has a lush, wool-like appearance and texture. Soft, durable, and stain-resistant, jute rugs are perfect for high-traffic areas.

Kilims These flat-weave reversible wool rugs have bold, intricate designs. Originally designed to be placed on sandy desert floors by nomadic peoples of countries such as Iran, Iraq, Pakistan, and Turkey, kilim rug patterns represent different tribes and regions. All are rich, vibrant, and geometric.

Leather Tanned animal hides make a durable upholstery option that gets softer and more beautiful with use. The surface texture, dimension, pigment regularity, and softness of the hide all distinguish high-quality leather. Black and brown are classic leather colors, but manufacturers now dye leathers in a range of hues. When dyed a bright yellow or cherry red, leather takes on a contemporary look.

Limestone Composed of the mineral calcite, limestone comes from the beds of evaporated seas and lakes. Because it is softer than many stones, limestone crumbles gently over time, becoming more beautiful with age.

Linen Woven from the fibers of the flax plant, linen can be as fine as a handkerchief or as substantial as canvas. Twice as strong as cotton, linen softens with washing. This versatile fabric is often used for tablecloths and upholstery. Lightweight linen curtains provide privacy while still allowing sunlight to shine through. Vintage pieces contribute a sense of history to a room's decor.

Loop cotton Naturally absorbent cotton rugs come in a range of surface textures, including loop. "Loop" refers to the pile of a tufted rug when the yarn is passed through the backing from back to front, then front to back, and the resulting loop is left intact. The loop can also be cut to create cut-loop cotton.

Mahogany This valuable, close-grained hardwood varies in color from golden brown to deep red brown and is used for the manufacture of fine furniture, cabinetry, paneling, interior trim, doors, decorative borders, and flooring.

Matelassé This double-woven fabric, named for the French word for "quilted," has raised decorative patterns on its surface that mimic the look of a quilt. The effect is achieved through the process of weaving in an interlocking wadding weft (a filling thread or yarn), rather than through quilting. A matelassé throw will become softer with repeated washings and adds warm texture.

Mies van der Rohe, Ludwig The German-born American architect Ludwig Mies van der Rohe (1886–1969), a founder of the International Style, is credited with the creation of the glass-and-steel modernist skyscraper. His furniture designs include the Barcelona chair, made of chrome-plated flat steel upholstered in leather. His oft-quoted dictum "Less is more" continues to influence designers today.

Milk paint A mix of casein (powdered milk protein), lime, and stable earth pigments, milk paint was used on house interiors and furniture by early American colonialists and Shakers. This environmentally friendly paint adheres easily to porous surfaces such as wood and dries quickly to a hard, flat finish that can be sanded, distressed, oiled, waxed, polished, or varnished. Its distinctive finish lends an antique look to new furnishings.

Mirrors The most common type of mirror is made of plate glass coated on one side with metal or some other reflective surface. Mirrors can make a room look bigger and amplify its light.

Mudroom Commonly located near the entry of a house or off the kitchen, this room is intended for the shedding of raingear, coats, and shoes. Well-designed storage is key to the creation of an easy-to-use, welcoming space.

Organdy This stiff, transparent fabric made of cotton or silk is commonly used for making curtains. It is available with patterns or in solid colors.

Oriental rugs Traditionally from countries such as China, India, Iran, and Turkey, these richly patterned, long-lasting wool rugs are usually hand-knotted or woven.

Pine This wood from coniferous trees (which produce cones) tends to be softer than wood from deciduous trees (which shed leaves). It is a popular choice for furniture, flooring, and cabinetry because of its rustic quality. Old pine is best for flooring; another option is a harder species such as white pine, a straight-grained wood with little resin that is often used for interior trim as well.

Quilt Patchwork may have been born of a necessity to recycle fabric scraps, but sewing together different fabrics soon became an American art form, predominantly practiced by women, and a traditional gift of love and remembrance. The top of a patchwork quilt is sewn from scraps or blocks of fabric. A whole-cloth quilt is a solid piece of fabric, which shows off intricate stitchery. A quilt can give a room a sense of tradition.

Rammed earth A mixture of earth, water, and cement is poured into molds and tamped down to create thick, highly compacted walls or floors. Termite- and fire-resistant, rammed-earth buildings are energy-efficient and suitable for all climates. Because their thermal mass slows the transfer of heat or cold, rammed-earth buildings stay warm in the winter and cool in the summer.

Raw silk Fabric or yarn made from untreated silk has a nubby feel and a low sheen. Raw silk's durability and gentle drape make it a good choice for curtains.

Redwood While any wood that produces a red dye is considered a redwood, the most famous are coast redwoods, which grow up to 360 feet in height. This durable hardwood is used in home interiors and exteriors, including decks, paneling, and furniture.

Rumford fireplace Classical and elegant, the Rumford fireplace was widely used in the early half of the nineteenth century. Tall and shallow to reflect more heat, it features a streamlined throat that efficiently removes smoke. It is named for its creator, Count Rumford (1753–1814).

Sailcloth A light, strong woven canvas originally used for making boat sails, sailcloth resists stretching, moisture, and tearing. It is a good fabric choice for hardwearing upholstery.

Samovar This type of urn has a spigot at its base. In Russia, it is traditionally used to boil water for tea.

Seagrass Commercially grown in China, seagrass produces a fiber that is similar to straw and smoother than coir, sisal, or jute. Its smooth surface and subtle green tone add warmth and an outdoors appeal. The fiber's rugged durability makes it suitable for high-traffic areas.

Shag rug These soft, deep-pile rugs with a "shaggy" surface were popular in the 1960s and '70s, and are being rediscovered for their comfort and casual style.

Sheepskin Long used for furnishings, especially fireside rugs, plush white sheepskin combines lush softness with rugged resilience, and adds texture to any room.

Shibori silk A process of hand-dyeing silk by controlling the dye flow through folds sewn into the fabric, this Japanese fabric art is often likened to tie-dyeing. However, shibori requires greater precision because silk is so absorbent.

Sisal A flexible fiber is made from the leaves of the sisal (or agave) plant, which grows in Africa and South America. Softer to the touch than coir, but still durable, sisal is commonly woven into flat rugs with an even, highly textural surface. Sisal rugs hide dirt, resist stains, and absorb sounds, making them practical in high-traffic areas, such as foyers.

Taffeta A crisp, smooth, plain-woven silk or linen fabric, taffeta is distinguished by its lustrous sheen. Although traditionally used for ball gowns and formal women's fashions, it's also an ideal choice for window treatments and table skirts.

Tartanware This genre of wooden items of everyday use were made in Scotland, from the early 1800s through 1933, and decorated with Scottish tartan patterns. These were later replicated on items like thermoses and lunchboxes. Today, both kinds are popular collectibles.

Ticking Originally used primarily to make mattress and pillow coverings, this strong, tightly woven cotton fabric features a characteristic pattern of simple stripes against a natural background. Today the term describes a variety of striped fabrics that have many uses in the home, from curtains to bed linens.

Twill This smooth, durable fabric is tightly woven, usually of cotton, and has a raised diagonal grain. Washable and relatively flat, this versatile weave is a good choice for slipcovers or upholstery in both summer and winter seasons. Denim and gabardine are examples of twill weaves. Brushed twill is finished to emphasize the fabric's soft nap.

Velvet Traditionally woven from wool, silk, or cotton, velvet has a raised pile, which consists of rows of loops that are cut to produce a fur-like texture. Used for draperies since the Middle Ages, velvet adds an elegant texture to furnishings. How well a velvet resists flattening depends on yarn quality and pile density.

Venetian glass The city of Venice has been a world-renowned center of glassmaking since the Middle Ages. Specialties include transparent, delicate *cristallo* glass, which is blown into intricate designs, and *lattimo,* or milk glass, an opaque white glass used to make elaborate patterns in clear glass.

Voile This lightweight, soft woven fabric is traditionally made from cotton or silk, but can also be made of wool or synthetic fibers. Light plays off its sheerness, so voile curtains make a room feel light-infused but not sunbaked.

Waffle-weave cotton Recessed squares give this knit fabric a honeycomb texture that breathes easily.

Wainscoting Originally developed to prevent wall damage in heavy-traffic areas, wainscoting usually refers to wooden boards or panels that cover the lower portion of a wall. The term can also refer to full-height wall paneling. Beadboard is the most common type of wainscoting.

Wicker Created by weaving flexible branches or twigs from plants such as bamboo, cane, rattan, reed, or willow around a coarser frame, wicker is commonly used to make durable baskets and furniture. Wicker baskets offer attractive storage. A durable material, wicker can stand up to a century of normal use.

Wrought iron Iron bar stock is forged or bent into shape to create decorative and architectural elements such as grates, furniture, wine racks, and stair railings. Decorative forms include Gothic tracery, plant forms, and classical motifs. Today, wrought iron is sometimes actually made of steel.

Index

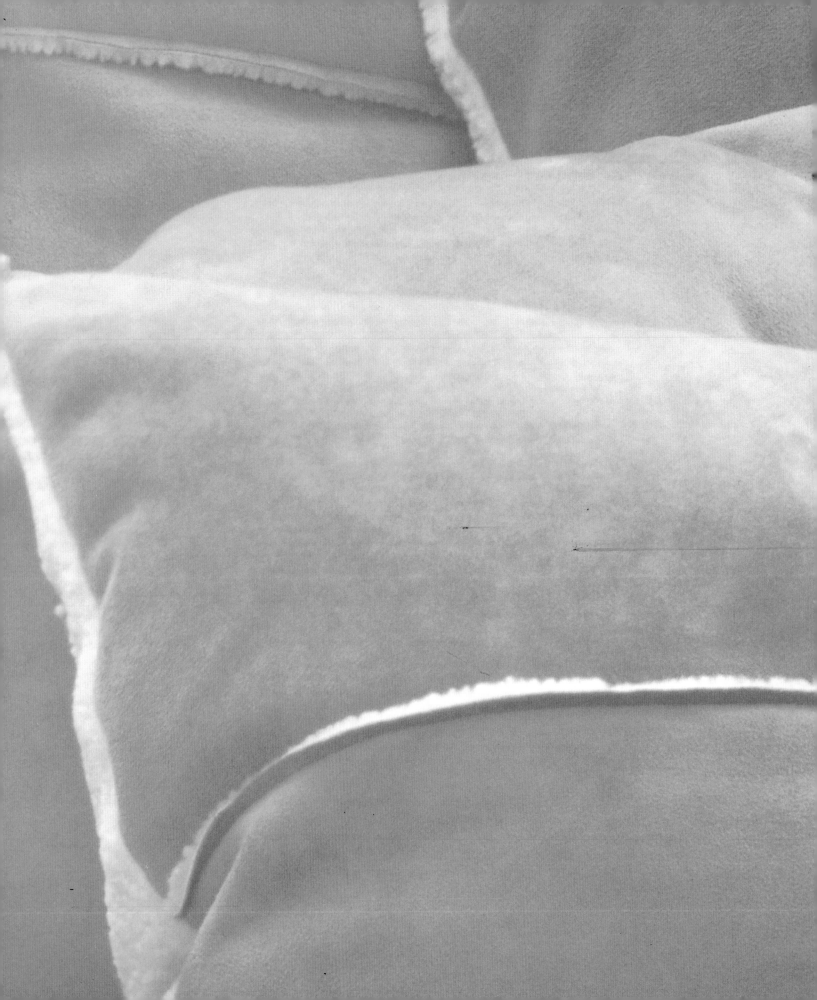